MW00898690

Country Joe and Me

By

Ron Cabral

With an Afterword by Country Joe McDonald

authorHOUSE

1663 LIBERTY DRIVE, SUITE 200
BLOOMINGTON, INDIANA 47403
(800) 839-8640
www.authorhouse.com

First published by AuthorHouse 03/31/04

ISBN: 1-4107-6538-5 (e)
ISBN: 1-4107-6537-7 (sc)
ISBN: 1-4184-0642-2 (dj)

Library of Congress Control Number: 2003110579

Printed in the United States of America
Bloomington, Indiana

This book is printed on acid-free paper.

Cover Design by Ralph Solonitz

CONTENTS

PREFACE

This is the story of two young Americans—Country Joe (Joe McDonald) and Me (Ron Cabral). We became deeply involved in some of the massive changes that were happening around us, both as participants and in some cases as guiding forces in the direction of some of the events. Our lives have continually crossed paths and intertwined through four decades of mutual tumultuous history involving a counter-cultural revolution, psychedelic music, war, political activism, and alternative education.

Our journey begins in 1960 as two eighteen-year olds meet up in the mysterious Far East 5,200 miles from home with no clue as to what the world & life had in store for them. What are the odds of two guys right out of high school ending up in Japan in the same small U.S. Navy unit, both assigned to the same barracks, both trained trombone players, both from California, both air controllers, and both with immigrant Russian Bolshevik grandmothers? Too many coincidences...too many planets lining up...something magical was in the works.

And the parallels have always kept showing up...hanging together in the Navy and then going our separate ways only to meet up again and again over the years. Suddenly it's 1963 and Joe arrives at my parent's house in San Francisco while he is on a Jack Kerouac like *On the Road* trip of sorts traversing the West Coast - all the way to Alaska and back to Southern California. Joe is soon to plant roots in the Bay Area.

...Fast-forward to 1967 and the world I thought I knew had turned upside down.

One of us is in the audience in Golden Gate Park at San Francisco's "Human Be-In" and accidentally spots the other on stage playing a tambourine - Joe had somehow turned into County Joe of Country Joe & The Fish. Then it was California Hall, The Avalon Ballroom and The Fillmore. Both of us become embroiled in the music and political revolution boiling over in San Francisco and Berkeley...one as the leader of an important rock band, musician and songwriter and the other as a public school teacher, band manager and occasional concert organizer...Good times and brawls with Bill Graham happen along the way...

While teaching at a public alternative high school (Opportunity High) I was able to bring Joe in as a volunteer teacher and he stuck around for almost two years. We teamed up to create a unique music education program in the school during the early 70's. Around the same time we both became family men with wives and numerous children to help raise—Joe's brood ranges in age from 35 to 12 mine from 36 to 28.

Joe always a rock star and folk singer eventually becomes a strong advocate for Vietnam Veterans causes. He is also a scholar on War Nurses and Florence Nightingale and he is also a leading interpreter of the songs and life of Woody Guthrie. I became a middle school principal and had a 35-year career in the San Francisco Schools. At the same time that I worked in the schools I was also a Photojournalist writing and taking photographs on maritime subjects for 20 years for Coast Guard magazines.

Joe continues to perform with vigor all over the USA and in Europe. He continues to write songs and release new recordings. I wrote this book because I believe strongly in Joe and that this story needed to be told, it is about my Navy buddy who eventually became Country Joe. It is also about some of the shared experiences we had in the military, in music and in education during the heat of the '60's and early '70's.

This story is history written from the inside. It is a biography, an autobiography and documentary about two people who lived it and also made it happen.

Ron Cabral
Concord, California
June 11, 2003

Joe and Ron. Photo by Kathy McDonald.

This book is dedicated to the memory of my parents Flora and Ernest Cabral also to the memory of Joe's parents Florence and Worden McDonald

1: RED DIAPER BABY

Washington, DC–1942

Joe was named after Joseph Stalin in the days before everyone realized that Stalin was an insane maniac. Joe was born January 1, 1942 in Washington, D.C. to Worden and Florence McDonald. Joe's parents were both on the left side of the ideological fence, and you could probably call them American communists if you wanted to throw around labels.

Joe's grandmother Bella Voronoff was a Russian-Jewish immigrant who had opposed the Czar in Russia in 1905. She and her sister Rose left Russia to seek a new life in America. Bella often took Joe's mom to political meetings in D.C. Oddly enough, Bella also became one of the first female truck drivers in the D.C. area.

Joe's father Worden McDonald grew up in Oklahoma during the Dust Bowl and the Depression era. He was a very adventurous young man who had gone to seek his fortune in Alaska. During the 30's, however, Worden began to participate in the American Labor Movement, and his politics took a turn for the left. A few years after his ideals jelled, he met and married Florence. It seemed a perfect match.

I met both Joe's parents in the late 60's after they finally moved to Berkeley from Southern California. I liked them right away

Baby Joe
Photo by Worden
McDonald

and they were always very friendly to me—Joe had introduced them to me as his Navy pal from Japan. After Joe began to work his way into the music industry, Joe's parents liked to reminisce and relive some of Joe's early musical leanings.

Worden said, "When Joe was about 10 years old, he played the harmonica, I would ask him if he could play a certain song, and he would always say no. But then he'd say 'well if you could whistle it for me I can play it.' Then he would just play it—I always thought that was pretty amazing."

Worden also said, "Joe began playing the trombone in school. He liked it right away and started practicing at least three hours a day at home. He got pretty good at it as time went along. When Joe got to high school he had a good sound—I enjoyed hearing him practice."

Besides excelling in music, Joe was also a good horseback rider as a youth in El Monte.

"It seemed that when he wasn't busy with guinea pigs, horses, rabbits or dogs he was taking a music lesson or practicing," said Joe's mother, Florence.

Joe grew up in the period during and right after World War II. The country and society was still in shock at the atrocities man could commit. "Joe was always a very sensitive child his music seemed his link to sanity," Florence said.

"When I was very young I learned from my mother about the death camps for Jews in World War II. My mother and I had many arguments about our heritage. I couldn't understand how we as non-believers and non-practicing Jews could have been killed for being Jewish if we had lived say in Germany or Russia during WWII."

"When the pogroms come they will find you," Joe's mother always said. Joe had nightmares about these things when he was very young. Joe had dreams about being taken away to concentration camps by boogiemen. He had a hard time with these dreams for a long time.

"Later in life, I realized that I was defined as a Jew by Jew haters not by myself. Also I came to realize that my mother was suffering from survivor guilt and post traumatic stress syndrome from her experience of being the child of Russian Jewish immigrants."

Most people do not grow up with the reality Joe experienced as a red diaper baby. The truth was that Joe's parent's politics filled some

American's with hate and anger. "It isn't fair to place that burden on children. Like so many others, I was forced to react to the situation inherited at birth. All red diaper babies know what I am talking about," said Joe.

Joe never cared much for the rhetoric or activities of the radical labor movement in which his parents were engrossed, according to Florence. She never seemed disappointed, and in fact, was very proud of the music bug that gripped Joe in his youth. "The music of the men and women struggling for a better life appealed to him," she said.

Florence McDonald went on to be elected to the Berkeley city council and served in that office for many years. Worden remained an activist around Berkeley and wrote a book called *An Old Guy Who Feels Good.* Joe even though he had disagreements with his parents from time to time always remained devoted to them.

Joe lived in El Monte in Southern California, from the ages of 5 to 17 in the time when no freeways went through the town. His father was a long time employee of Bell Telephone in downtown LA, but he loved to play farmer in their quarter acre homestead by having a nice garden and animals. Those days gave Joe a real love and appreciation for animals.

Joe had a special horse named Rebel. They never used a bit on him because it hurt his mouth. Joe liked to ride him bareback. One day Worden rode Rebel to pick up Joe after school. Joe had his trombone with him, and he climbed up behind his father with the trombone case hanging alongside the horse. On the way home Worden decided to let Rebel experience meeting a train at a railroad crossing. The train started coming and as it got closer, its whistle grew louder and louder. Rebel started jumping around while Worden tried in vain to control the horse.

Joe held on to his father as he fought the animal that got more agitated and tried to rear up. Joe slid off with his trombone when he finally got the opportunity. With Joe off the horse, Worden got the animal under control. After that though, Rebel didn't seem to mind trains at all.

Joe had a number of harrowing experiences on the back of a horse while growing up. Joe was riding Rebel bareback in his small back yard one day, and he brought the horse to a brisk canter. The canter was a crazy move, as Joe's yard was such a small area with a garden, some fruit trees and a garage all crammed into a small area. Joe suddenly lost control and slipped off Rebel falling down his side, bouncing off his chest, and landing flat on his back on the ground in front of him. Joe looked up to see a hoof coming right down on his face. At that point Rebel looked Joe straight in the eyes and lifted his hoof out of the way and hopped over him. Joe always said Rebel was a good horse.

Joe and I have shared ancestry when it comes to communist Russia.

My grandmother, Thelma Gorbonoff, and her family also fled Czarist Russia in 1906-07. At that time men were conscripted for 25-year hitches for the Czar's Army. They were poor peasants living in Siberia near the town of Chita, when they decided to flee and head east towards Harbin, Manchuria. They loaded up all the horse-drawn wagons they could find and drove across the Siberian plains much like the pioneer's of the old west did crossing along the Oregon Trail. If both

Joe's and my family hadn't fled, we certainly would not have had as much fun in the 60's.

After a huge ordeal they arrived in Harbin to hear of jobs in a place called Hawaii. Dole Pineapple Company had sent recruiters out to Harbin to try and hire white labor to work in the fields in Hawaii. It was a time of racism and "yellow peril" fears in Hawaii. They offered the Russians one ruble a day if they agreed to make the long sea voyage to Honolulu. My grandmother's family signed up.

As they were boarding a ship in Korea for the trip to Hawaii via Japan, Thelma's younger brother, a 10-year-old boy, disappeared at dockside. His disappearance was noted just as the ship had cast lines and was headed out. Screams for the Captain to stop went unheard from the distraught Russians in steerage. The boy Vasily was never found or heard from again.

After years of working in the fields of Hawaii, Thelma met a Portuguese-American sailor named Charles Cabral who worked on the San Francisco-Honolulu run for Matson Lines. They fell in love, married and Charles took Thelma to a better life in San Francisco. They lived for years on Potrero Hill, a working class neighborhood with stunning views of the San Francisco Bay. I often visited her there when she was in her last years and heard her stories of how she came to America. She felt the Czar was a rat the way he treated the people and in her mind Joe Stalin saved Russia. She was sad when Stalin died in 1953. I watched her cry while watching Stalin's funeral on TV. Neither Russian Orthodox nor Jewish, she was connected someway to the Molokan Sect, a type of holy-roller Christian congregation that settled along the

West Coast from Seattle to Baja California. There was a large contingent of Molokans who settled on Potrero Hill. Illiterate in both English and Russian she lived to age 94 and is buried in Seaside, California.

Ron in 1943.
Photo from Ron Cabral collection.

My father Ernest Cabral was born in Hawaii in 1914. He arrived in San Francisco in 1918 with Thelma and grew up on Potrero Hill. He lived there till he married my mother Flora Martinez in 1940—I came along a year later. Flora had come to San Francisco as a 5-year old immigrant from Costa Rica in 1924 with her mother Sara and brother Claude. Ernest and Flora met during the Depression era of the 1930's while Flora was attending Mission High. My father served in the Civilian Conservation Corps (CCC) after he graduated from Commerce High in 1933. In those days a young man had pretty much only two choices—enlist in the Army for $21.00 per month or join the CCC for $30.00—there were few other jobs. Ernest was assigned to a road building crew in the remote forests of Modoc County in Northern California. He later became a career civilian employee of the U.S. Army as an overseas supply specialist at Fort Mason and the Oakland Army Terminal. My mother operated her own beauty shop for 35 years in the city.

While Joe was attending Arroyo High School in El Monte, he became totally obsessed with music. Fourteen-year-old Joe mastered the techniques for playing the trombone. At the same time he learned the acoustic guitar, and he was developing his vocal and song writing talents. From 1955 to 1957, Joe was a member of the school concert band, which played mainly, marches, and modern pieces by composers like Aaron Copeland and Richard Rogers. Joe often fell asleep with the radio on tuned to LA stations that played Little Richard, Chuck Berry, Buddy Holly, Ritchie Valens, Fats Domino, Elvis, Jerry Lee Lewis and others. Joe also played in a Dixieland jazz band, and he had become familiar with the works of Jack Teagarden, Dave Breubeck, Turk Murphy and J.J. Johnson. Since Joe was also a member of the school marching band, he had to go to all the football games and run up and down the field at half time playing Souza marches. Sometimes after marching, he would go straight home to rehearse his own rock and roll band. Young Joe was living a very real musical life—he was experiencing music of all types all at once.

Joe got his first money gig while still in high school. A friend got him a gig, playing trombone in a dance band. The band had 15 pieces and played tunes like "Star Dust", "Deep Purple" and "Moon Glow."

"My parents always had music on at home," said Joe. "I heard lots of Gilbert and Sullivan with Spike Jones, Woody Guthrie and Pete Seeger thrown in." On weekends Joe would go to the El Monte American Legion Stadium to see Fats Domino, and Johnny Otis.

Joe at Arroyo High School 1958.
McDonald family archives.

As a senior in high school, Joe decided to put his first band on the road. The band was called The Nomads. The band was made up of one guitar, a snare drum, a sax and vocals. There was no bass player. The Nomads soon broke up and Joe started his second band called The Tanganyika Trio. The trio was a kind of calypso band with congas and bongos. They did a few gigs in Orange County and in Pasadena at some folksy bohemian type coffee houses of the late 50's.

The trio lasted for four months until right after Joe graduated from Arroyo at age 17. Joe's third band was a little different from The Nomads and The Tanganyika Trio—that band was The San Diego Naval Station Recruit Drum and Bugle Corps. This time Joe was a bugler and not the leader of a rock or calypso band. Joe being a highly proficient trombone player had no trouble learning to play a bugle. Joe could easily have ended up playing in a Navy band, but for some reason he was assigned to Naval Aviation and soon found himself off to Navy Air Control School in Olathe, Kansas. He was somewhat disappointed as he thought he was going to be sent to Signalman School. When he arrived at Olathe he spent a month cleaning out large pots at the base mess hall.

2: IN THE NAVY

Atsugi, Japan - 1960

When Joe arrived at U.S. Naval Air Station, Atsugi, Japan in May of 1960 he looked around at the place that would be his new home for the next two years. Right out of boot camp and air control school, he had never been to a foreign country, and Atsugi, 40 miles west of Yokohama near Mt. Fuji, was as foreign as it gets to a 18-year-old from California.

The base buzzed with fighter and attack planes from the big carriers that sat offshore. There was always a new carrier operating in the area. Carriers like the Ticonderoga, Bon Homme Richard (Bonnie Dick), Hornet, Ranger, Oriskany and others launched their aircraft to Atsugi, and then tied up for liberty at Yokosuka Naval Base.

I looked up from behind my desk in the pilot flight schedules office when I first laid eyes on the new arrival to our unit. Our office took care of pilot flight logs, issued Notice to Airmen, handed out maps, and maintained flight schedules. At the time I thought very little about Joe as I finally gave him the tidbit of information he needed before he saw the chief for check in. "Just listen and don't say anything," I said, winking at him as he shuffled off down the passageway.

Bowman spent his days as the man in charge of the air control tower operator unit. You could tell from his age and attitude that Chief

Bowman was one of those rare sailors who totally loved the Navy. The chief often said the Navy pulled him out of the gutter and gave him a home when he was a kid of 18. Bowman was also a vehement anti-communist constantly worried about the commies in Russia, China, North Korea and elsewhere that were trying to take over the world. He raved constantly about it to anyone who listened.

Joe the Sailor
Courtesy McDonald
Family Archives

So, it surprised me little when he returned an hour later talking about the chief raving about "commie whores" in the bars in town. I looked up blankly, and he finally introduced himself as "Joe McDonald from El Monte, California."

We made small talk and then the subject turned to music. Joe went on to say he mainly liked folk music and that he really enjoyed the Kingston Trio, Harry Belafonte, Little Richard and Richie Valens. Joe also mentioned that he played trombone.

I had just had my trombone shipped over to me from San Francisco and it was in the flight simulator building across the street from the tower. An odd looking and distinct sounding instrument, the trombone has killed more friendships, potential dates and conversations than it ever helped. At the time I met Joe, high school band had none of the stigma of today, but that fear of trombone reprisal still weighed on each of us. So being two admitted trombone-playing Californian's was enough to guarantee we would spend much time together during our tour of duty.

Joe asked me to show him around the operations building, especially the control tower. We soon went up into the tower, and I introduced him around to the air control petty officers on duty. Joe showed an immediate interest and excitement in his future job. "I can't wait to get on the duty rotation," he told the duty crew. A few of the disgruntled Navy petty officers stopped their activity for a nano-second to gape at Joe.

Joe said, "I sure do love to watch those Navy and Marine planes take off and land." It is always easier to make excited comments when you're the new guy.

The barracks we lived in were built by the U.S. Navy Seabee's (the Navy's construction battalion) right after the U.S. Occupation of Japan began right after WW II ended in 1945—they had been remodeled some in the 50's. Our particular barracks was organized into partitions so that numerous men shared three high bunks and each man had a fairly good-sized personal locker. The head was a long walk away from the bunk areas with a row of 12 gleaming urinals and 12 toilets without stalls, doors or any other methods of privacy—this changed after a few months as stalls were finally added.

The sinks were often full of multi-colored bugs each morning during the warmer weather. Beetles, worm-like creatures and various crawlies disappeared after running the water for a few minutes, but the next morning they were all back. Showers were often packed with sailors.

The Navy seemed to have an unwritten zero privacy rule. In a shower filled with guys, there were usually more tattoos than people. Many sailors made the mistake of having their girl friends name put on their arm only to eventually get the "Dear John, I found someone else" or "I can't wait anymore" letter. Those letters called for a trip back to the tattoo parlor to have "Mom" or some other design tattooed over the name. And always there was music playing in the barracks; country music like Johnny Cash singing "I Walk the Line" played over and over.

Two Japanese houseboys kept the barracks spotless. The houseboys made up the bunks each morning, waxed and buffed the floors, shined shoes and took out and picked up laundry. Some of the barracks workers fought in the Japanese military during the War, it was an odd arrangement. Every month each sailor would chip in $5.00 as a tip for the workers.

We were both 18. I had been at the base a few months, so when Joe first arrived, he and I walked the base to show him some of the sights. The base was very famous because it had been a Kamikaze training center during WWII. General Douglas MacArthur landed at Atsugi in 1945 on his way to take the Japanese surrender on the deck of the battleship U.S.S Missouri in Tokyo Bay. The base chapel was actually a former Buddhist temple that was used by the Kamikaze pilots during their training.

It was a common procedure to register your religious preferences with the chaplain when arriving on base. On one of our walks, Joe and I stopped off to do just that—I can't recall what religion Joe registered. In boot camp dog tags were issued and a religion was stamped on it.

Joe asked the chaplain if he knew of any orphanages or places that would like to hear some American folk music—Joe was already looking for a gig and had somehow just acquired a guitar. The chaplain said he would let us know if he heard of anything but he had a sort of rueful look in his eye.

Our conversations seemed to always come back to music...or women. Joe asked, "Do you know anybody who likes to make music around here?"... "Do you know any girls out in town?"...What are some of the real good bars?"

A sailor named Larry Parmenter heard Joe play some guitar out on the barracks fire escape one evening and told Joe he had a small recording system put together with a good tape recorder and speakers over in the Link Trainers (flight simulator) shack. Larry invited some of us over for a jam session. It wouldn't take long before we would be there and on a regular basis.

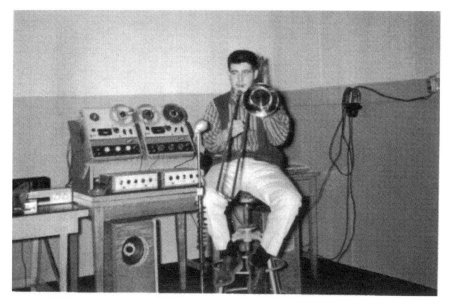

Ron on Trombone at Atsugi, Japan 1960.
Photo by Larry Parmenter.

There was much to see on the base, and many months passed for most of the new guys before they were able to see even half. A young sailor first arriving might see some U-2 aircraft flying out of Atsugi. The controversial U-2 spy plane made big news in 1960 as pilot Gary Powers was shot down over the Soviet Union and had been captured as a U.S. spy. The day before that made the news I saw one take off—it just went straight up like a rocket and disappeared—the U2's had been flying out of Atsugi for a long time. After Powers was shot down (he did not fly out of Atsugi) the U.S. had to admit to the fact that it had been spying on Russia and other countries for a long time with the high altitude spy plane.

One evening we went to the EM or "Enlisted Man's" club. The club had a massage parlor manned by several young Japanese women and slot machines in the lobby, just like in Vegas or Reno. "Happy Hour" was from 7 to 8 p.m., and all drinks cost a dime. Since there was no limit on ordering, it was not uncommon for a sailor to order a dozen whiskey sours or beers at one time, and just sit there ingesting them until they were gone. After a night of drinking, the sailor would often pass out, get dragged back to the barracks by his mates and thrown into his rack. Sailors woke, vomited and passed out again throughout the night often coating the floor with puke.

A few nights later we went over to the EM club to see the singing legends The Mills Brothers. A Japanese swing band, and a singer called the Japanese Nat King Cole were also appearing. The place was packed, but the Brothers were an hour late. By the time they started singing "Glow Worm" it was too late. Most of the sailors were blind drunk and made so much noise the legends could not be heard past the first row. The Mills Brothers got upset and left early so the Japanese Nat King Cole impersonator had to come on sooner than he expected. Right after that a Japanese 40's style dance band started playing Tommy Dorsey and Glenn Miller style tunes. The base clubs always put on great shows drawing both name U.S. talent and local talent from the Tokyo-Yokohama area. We just took it all for granted. Bob Hope even appeared at the base once while we were there but I recall being on duty that night so I missed seeing him.

During a break Joe asked one of the trombone players and the bandleader if he could sit in on a song or two. They hesitated, but finally said yes. Joe walked to the section and took the trombone. The band started to play, and Joe didn't even hesitate. He put the mouthpiece to his lips, still warm from the other guy blowing on it, and joined in on "Perfidia" then "Pennsylvania 6-5000." Joe could really blow that horn—he had a great tone and could really project that t-bone sound.

The sailors hardly noticed. A couple of sober fellows in the audience who were close enough to hear perked up at the sound of Joe's jazzy playing, but for the most part, Joe's Japanese debut went unnoticed. After the set, Joe handed the trombone back to its owner who looked at the thing like he had never seen it before.

In 1960 any sailor regardless of age could drink all manner of alcohol every night. Some became full-blown alcoholics before reaching 20 years old. If they were not drinking on base, then they were in town drinking at the bars, which is precisely what Joe and most of us did every chance we could. Joe and some of the guys from the barracks often headed out to the nearest town Sagami-Otsuka. The town was 2 miles from the base and could best be reached by bus or cab. Rice paddies surrounded the town, and with rice paddies came the smell of human fertilizer.

Small tank trucks with suction hoses would drain out the wastes collected from each houses septic tank in the area and deliver the stuff to a processor who added chemicals to it and sprayed it directly on the rice paddies. By the heat of August the smell was at its peak. This practice of using human wastes has been going on for thousands of years in Japan, but the strangest thing was the base had a huge 18-hole golf course that buttressed right up to a wire fence separating the golf course from the rice paddies. Some times the golfers and the rice farmers would look at each other through the fence—they would just sort of stare at each other with that god-awful stench hanging in the air.

Sagami-Otsuka looked like a town out of the old American west. It boasted dirt streets and over fifty bars that could pass for western movie set saloons. The town also had two or three hotels (the best being the Cherry Hotel), a few small country style houses, and a train station with service to Tokyo and Yokohama. Each bar was run by a mama-san that employed eight to ten young women who hustled drinks...and their bodies after closing time.

These were the same women that Chief Bowman warned Joe and everyone else on base about. He said that many of them were not Japanese, but they were North Korean spies and they only wanted to collect secrets about base activities. I still don't know if that was true, or if it was just Bowman's paranoia.

The women would take a sailor to a hotel or nearby house for the night for less than $10.00 or about 3,600 Yen. Sometimes they would have sex for free if the sailor would promise to bring them cigarettes and other goods from the Base Exchange—a carton of cigarettes cost $1.00 in 1960.

Venereal disease was a problem at the base and the common procedure was to put the man who came down with it on restriction for two weeks and prescribe anti-biotics. Then the afflicted sailor would have to go the base security office and identify the picture of the woman he may have been with from a certain bar. The base security office had binders for each bar in town containing photos of all the bar workers. A Japanese health inspector would then go out to the bar and issue her a ticket for a required health examination. The woman with the disease would then disappear for a spell while being treated.

The different venereal diseases were a painful and difficult experience to cope with—especially under the Navy "no privacy" blanket. Any pressure or constrictions of the private area proved painful. So, sometimes a sailor with a bad case of some STD often removed the mattress off a bottom rack and lay naked and face down on the springs allowing his genitals to hang through soaking it in a vial of some kind of blue fluid. In those days there were various strange treatments for sailors who had some forms of VD or non-specific urethritis (NSU) or shankers as the medics didn't really know what remedies to use or how to cure the maladies exactly. Whenever a Marine Unit in transit was passing through Atsugi the cases of VD skyrocketed. Many of these units had just come from exotic locations and they brought unknown bugs with them.

Once off restriction some sailor's celebrated by having a new shark-skin suit tailored for $50 by a shop right outside the base. It was common to see young sailors nattily dressed, some wearing cashmere overcoats for a night on the town. Along the road to town there were open sewers or benjo ditches. Occasionally a sailor with a new suit was found face down and drunk in a benjo ditch by the shore patrol. It was a sorry site to see the SP's pulling a mud-soaked sailor out of one of those ditches during a rainstorm at midnight.

Joe in barracks at Atsugi 1961 with Bill Gregory
and two Japanese Self-Defense force pals.
Photo by Ron Cabral.

I met a few interesting guys from the base, and we eventually became friends. Joe, Larry, Bill Gregory, Henry Butler and I spent a lot of time together. Joe started playing the guitar he had somehow acquired more and more in the barracks and everyone enjoyed his singing and playing. Larry continued to encourage Joe and some of us to keep coming to his shop for the jam sessions, which were starting to sound good. Bill, Larry and I joined in on bongos, trombone, mandolin, and on back-up vocals. Joe conducted the sessions like a real rehearsal and we all had a great time. Joe kept saying he wanted to take our little act on the road and perform for the kids in orphanages, but we never heard further from the chaplain so that never happened.

Mainly we just had fun with the playing and singing. After we played music Larry would let us all fly the Link Trainers, flight simulator machines called the blue boxes, for a couple of hours. He would give us maps to practice approaches to various airports we never heard of like Saigon and to airports in Laos and Cambodia. This was the first time I had ever heard of Vietnam or Saigon.

Larry, an electronic wizard type, would be the simulated ground control approach (GCA) operator and would guide us in for a landing as if we were in IFR or instrument conditions. He would say things like," turn left to 270 degrees and descend to 4,000 feet, steady on-glide path, on-glide path." While flying the Link Trainers we all began to hear about this place called Saigon and this was in the middle of 1960. Since most of us were air control people it was good training to fly the blue boxes especially under the guidance of a Link Trainer tech.

While sitting at the Bar Rose in Sagami-Otsuka, I asked Joe why he joined the Navy. "I once saw a recruiting poster in downtown El Monte of a sailor holding up some signal flags on a ship - that image really had an impact on me to join up," Joe said. "I thought I could really sail the seven seas and maybe even get laid in every port." Soon two very friendly bar hostesses came and sat next to us and asked us to buy them drinks—we gladly did. We were very cool sailors.

The bargirls really liked the sailors who were going to be stationed at Atsugi for a long time. Those sailors became access to all kinds of benefits for the girls. Some permanently assigned sailors had several different girl friends for as long as they were stationed at Atsugi. The girls called these sailors "Skive Honchos." Many Japanese women hoped to marry a local sailor and go to live in the land of the big **PX—** the USA.

Many sailors did try to marry a girl they met in a bar. For some it was love at first sight. Most of the young men had never been around any highly sexual women like the bar workers they met in Sagami-Otsuka.

Ron and Sagami-Otsuka Bar Girl
Photo by Larry Parmenter

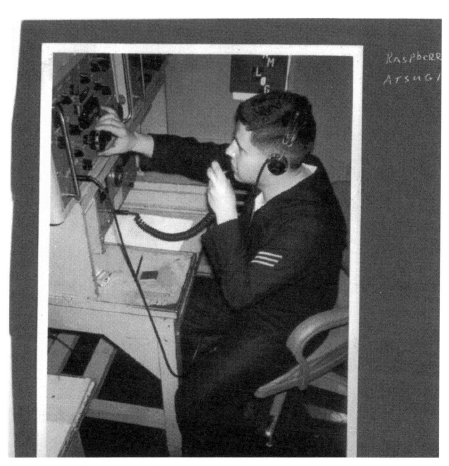

Ron on Raspberry Atsugi 1960. Photo by Bill Gregory.

In early 1961 news came that the runway at Atsugi was going to be closed for three months for repairs and some of us base permanent personnel were being transferred for short-term duty to nearby bases. I was sent to an Army base called Camp Zama, and Joe was sent to the Mito Gunnery Range at the east end of Tokyo Bay. Mito was used mainly by the Air Force for target practice. Every day dozens of jet fighters would shoot up the place and it was Joe's job to keep track of the hits and misses and report those scores to the flight leader-circling overhead. While he was in Mito he fell in love with a young Japanese woman about his own age named Toshie. They met in Yokohama when Joe was off-duty. They started living together briefly and he wanted to marry her.

During this time I did not see Joe.

As it turned out Joe finally left Mito and returned to the Operations Division at Atsugi. He saw Toshie for the last time just before he ended his tour of duty in Japan. His request for marriage was flatly denied by his commanding officer on the grounds that Joe was too young, and he was not capable of supporting a wife. Joe never said anymore about this to me.

The Navy had a well-kept secret policy of not allowing most marriage requests made by young sailors. They really were trying to prevent "old hookers" from taking advantage of 17 and 18-year-old naïve sailors. There were many cases of 18-year-old sailors falling in love with the first bar girl they had sex with. For many it was the first time, and they fell deeply in love right away. Marriage seemed a logical step.

El Monte (Calif.) HERALD—Thursday, October 13, 1960

McDonald Ends Naval Training In Air Control

EL MONTE — "Uncle Josh" and his nephew, Wordon McDonald, well known columnist of the El Monte and Valley Herald, recently celebrated the news of Joseph A. McDonald's completion of air controlman school at the Naval Air Station, Olathe, Kans.

Young McDonald is an airman apprentice. His parents reside at 11332 McGirk St. Worden McDonald, the air-man's father, is writer of the Herald garden feature, "Valley Gardening with Uncle Josh."

Airman McDonald was trained as approach controller for air control towers of the Navy air stations and for aircraft carriers at sea.

Early Bird Specials

Clipping from Hometown Newspaper 1960

JOE MCDONALD AT THE "BOMB DODGERS CLUB"

Petty Officer Joe McDonald at The Bomb Dodger Club – the enlisted club at Mito Gunnery Range 1961. From the Joe McDonald and Bruce Jensen Collection.

One evening two Shore Patrol men came roaring into the barracks at Atsugi looking for an 18-year-old sailor from Seattle by the name of Jim Weston. Weston had just turned in his application for marriage to the base commander. He was in love with a 45-year-old bar girl who may have met the occupation troops in 1945. The SP shined a flashlight in his face, yanked him out of the rack, ordered him to get dressed and pack his sea bag. One of the SP's read Weston his transfer orders saying, "As the Navy was looking out for your best interest you are ordered to report immediately to Sand Point, Washington for further duty." His designated plane was warming up as they spoke at the base airport terminal, and was going to leave in 20 minutes.

Weston freaked out and began yelling and screaming every curse imaginable. He threw himself against lockers and waved his arms around like a lunatic. The two SP's grabbed him and his sea bag and dragged him down the stairs to a waiting van—Weston cried, screaming and begged all the way down the stairs. A group of startled sailors, me among them, gathered at the top of the stairs watching - I never even got a chance to say goodbye to him.

It was now mid 1961, and Joe was back at Atsugi. Joe seemed like a different guy—he could have been down about having his marriage request rejected. He kept to himself more, appeared somewhat depressed and did not go out to town with the boys like he did before going to Mito. Joe was assigned to work in the operations office passing out flight maps to pilots, working the ship-to-shore radio called Raspberry Atsugi and he was being trained to become a flight dispatcher. We all really liked the ship-to-shore radio. We could hear propaganda messages in English coming out of Red China, Vladivostok, Russia, and North Korea saying things like, "Imperialist warmonger Eisenhower said today, blah, blah, blah, today..." and so on. We would also get messages from ships at sea. It was very exciting to hear broadcasts from so far away. On occasion we would get to transmit a message over Raspberry and that always seemed exciting.

Finally Joe got the call to start training for work in the control tower. He had been well trained for that duty, as he was a graduate of the Navy air control tower operator school in Olathe, Kansas. At Olathe he learned air navigation, meteorology, air traffic control procedures, radio communications, air traffic rules and FAA flight regulations. I never went to that school because I had come on active duty as a Reservist, but I was already on the tower crew as an air control striker, someone who learns on the job. I had managed to convince the tower chief to take me as a "striker" as I was a qualified Navy Airman and I also had taken some private flying lessons in single-engine seaplanes in Sausalito, California prior to coming on active duty. I looked forward to Joe joining us.

I was always amazed about how much responsibility the Navy gives its young sailors. Soon after I started in the tower I found myself on the "A" stand giving landing instructions to an entire squadron of jet fighters that were inbound from one of the carriers. "A" stand is the lead position in the tower and the "A" stand operator gives permission for all planes to take off and land. Not only were the fighters coming in but other aircraft as well so that there were as many as 50 planes in the flight pattern at one time. I was able to do this without a lot of problems as I had a kind of knack for this kind of work and pressure. This training helped me years later keep my cool as a public school teacher and administrator.

The first day Joe went to the tower he was put right on "A" stand. Joe had some problems making quick decisions, and he even froze up at times. The watch petty officer took him off and assigned him other duties hoping Joe would observe and learn the needed techniques. After two weeks he was sent back down to the operations office and back to dispatch and the Raspberry Atsugi radio.

"I had a hard time competing with those older tower guys," Joe confided in me. "I'm glad to be out of there, I made mistakes that could have killed somebody."

Like most sailors eventually do, Joe began to sour on his Navy career. He began to look forward to his discharge date. He did flirt with re-enlisting briefly at one point as many sailors do, but quickly came to his senses that he was no lifer.

When my day came for release from active duty in late 1961 I said goodbye to all my friends in the barracks, I invited them all to look me up when they got out, and I gave Joe a fan and a lighter with Atsugi engraved on it. I wondered if we would ever meet again—I really didn't think we ever would.

When my plane lifted off the runway at Tachikawa Air Force Base taking me home to San Francisco, I felt deeply saddened leaving my comrades, Japanese friends and the "Land of the Rising Sun" behind. I had no idea what was in store for me, or even the world, as we all headed full tilt into the 60's.

Souvenir lighter— "sayonara"

Ron the Sailor.
Photo from Ron Cabral collection.

3: BACK IN THE USA

San Francisco—1963 -1965

I had been out of the Navy almost two years, and I had not heard from Joe during any of that time. Then in the summer of 1963, I got a 4 a.m. phone call from Joe.

"Hey Ron," I had not an intelligent reply, all I could manage was a slurred "what's up Joe."

"I'm on my way up to Canada maybe even Alaska, ya wanna hang out?" Turns out, Joe was with a small black dog and two Englishmen, Nigel and Mike, a couple of hitchhikers he picked up on his way to San Francisco. Joe said he was traveling around California, and that he was headed for Portland, Vancouver and maybe even Alaska to play some clubs and any other places that featured folk music...his story got more interesting as he told me that on the way to San Francisco he had worked for a while at a Central Valley tomato farm lumping tomato boxes onto trucks for $1.08 per hour. He then said he planned to make the trip to Alaska in a rusty '49 green Ford coupe. I was then a sophomore at City College of San Francisco and was living on 24th Street in Noe Valley, so I immediately invited Joe and his newfound hitchhiker friends to come on over. I had not seen Joe since we both

Joe with his parents and younger Brother Billy.
photo by Nancy McDonald.

got out of the Navy and I was sure anxious to see him even if it was the middle of the night. By 5:00 a.m. we were all sitting in the kitchen drinking coffee and smoking cigarettes. Joe was full of stories about the farm worker experience he had just had and life on the road. Joe was really having a Kerouac type *On the Road* experience. The hitchhikers told me they were just biding their time till they could raise enough money to go to Hong Kong to open up a bar.

I was then living in the family five-bedroom house above my mother's beauty shop called "La Florita's House Of Beauty." One of the problems about living above a beauty shop is that the fumes from permanent wave solutions permeate through the walls and smell up the entire house. I can remember as a teen-ager going down stairs to the beauty shop with some of my buddies late at night. We would turn on the huge hair dryers full blast and then sit under them, smoking cigarettes, and reading the latest movie magazines. After that we would go into the back room and play an old upright piano. These were just some of the joys of living above a beauty salon in the heart of the inner city.

Joe and I quickly caught up on what had been happening in our lives to that point, and somehow the conversation turned to our fami-

34

lies. It was during this conversation that Joe told me that he was named after Joseph Stalin—this was the first time I had heard of this. Joe's mother, he went on, was the strongest Marxist in the family and she was very articulate about her politics. "I got my politics from my mom, but I got my dad's work ethic," he said. Joe's parents gave him a real understanding of the differences between communism and capitalism at a very young age.

His parents had a large impact on Joe's music choices. Folk music was always playing in Joe's home while he was growing up in Southern California. "Folk music had a huge influence on me," Joe said. I was surprised at how much Joe had been influenced by his parents, because he hardily mentioned them, or much about his childhood, when we were stationed together in the Navy.

Joe and the two hitchhikers stuck around my place for about a week. I took them out sight seeing all around the city. We cruised San Francisco in a blue Ford panel truck that I used for my part-time job delivering library books to merchant ships tied up at San Francisco and Oakland piers. Joe thought the San Francisco summer fog that draped around Twin Peaks and then just poured down into Noe Valley looked like Martian gas. The sight of the fog rolling down the flanks of Twin Peaks, like it does, is really something to behold. As a kid I always loved to watch the fog come in. I thought everyone had fog to watch—I didn't know I was living in a fairyland like setting, which Noe Valley can be when the climate is just right. There is no place quite like it anywhere.

Joe and I continued to catch up on each other's lives that week as we toured the city. Joe told me it was weird going back to El Monte after the Navy. He felt out of sorts, he said. His Navy time had made him a total neat freak, so he would walk around the family home inspecting it for dust and clutter. He made his bed so a quarter would bounce off it and he took lots of showers. He was acutely aware of order and structure.

Joe signed up to attend the local junior college, Mount San Antonio in Pomona. Since Joe had lived abroad and served a tour in the Navy, he found most the students were younger, and less mature than he was, and what was worse, none of the people he met at the college had ever served in the military or had ever been outside of California. Most of them seemed boring to Joe.

The world was slipping into full '60's mode, so Joe wanted to expand his mind and experience what the world had to offer. He went after his education hoping to accomplish his life altering epiphany, what ever that might have been, but all he found was a bunch of poorly taught, non- inspiring classes. Joe dropped out and got a job selling vacuum cleaners door to door.

His vacuum cleaner gig did not provide the moneymaking opportunity he had hoped for and it turned out to be a total disaster. Joe decided to finally take the plunge and become a folk singer.

I decided to call another Navy pal from Atsugi, Larry, who lived in Portland. "Joe's coming your way," I said. "Make sure and look out for him. He is with a couple of wanna be Bar owners, and who knows who else he'll pick up between here and Portland."

36

Turns out Joe made it to Portland, and Larry's place without much fuss. Larry was glad to see Joe, and he continued the Navy connection by calling another buddy of ours, Bill Gregory, who lived in the Seattle area. Bill came down to Portland, and the trio began looking for gigs for Joe to play.

Larry and Bill found a club in Portland that featured new talent. Larry talked to the very up-tight owner who agreed, reluctantly, to let Joe on stage. Larry told the guy Joe played the guitar and harmonica at the same time and was something like Bob Dylan. After just two numbers, the owner called Joe off the stage and told him to leave. Apparently, he didn't approve of a certain civil rights song Joe was singing. "I don't allow race music in here," the old red neck bellowed before kicking

The Berkeley String Quartet
From McDonald Family Archives

Joe out. Joe left Portland quite discouraged, and he and his two riders headed further north hoping to find work on a fishing boat. Joe fired up the old Ford and made it all the way to the Alaska border. Joe, Nigel and Mike soon found work in a fish packing plant in a small fishing village. Shortly after arriving in Alaska the Englishmen parted ways with Joe. Seems that the chaps did not like the work and they were soon laid off for slacking off. The boss also told Joe to take a hike. Joe then found a job in Ketchikan on a salmon fishing boat - a Purse

Seiner. He was aboard for a month of serious fishing and working in the galley. When the boat came in Joe sold his car and finally decided to head on back home to El Monte.

I didn't hear from Joe for another year. In early 1964, I was a senior at San Francisco State working on my BA and teaching credential. I had decided to go into teaching early in life, it was a dream or a calling I had as a kid while attending James Lick Junior High in San Francisco. I also wanted to be a pilot in the Navy in the worse way but that one just never quite worked out.

The doorbell rang—it was Joe. He stood at the front door, along side the "House of Beauty", with his new bride, Kathe Werum. Joe looked really different to me. He had a huge mustache and longish hair. "Ron, I've come to Frisco to break into show biz," he said, Kathe was about Joe's size and she wore round wire rimmed glasses. I was happy to see Joe and Kathe and set them up in my brother's vacant bedroom upstairs as he had just shipped out on the aircraft carrier Kitty Hawk. I had no idea Joe had gotten hitched and it really surprised me. I remembered that he almost got married only a few years before this in Japan in 1961.

He seemed really serious about it, the show biz thing; it made perfect sense to me, as I knew he had the required talent. I spent a few days with the newly wed's driving them around different neighborhoods of the city hoping to find an apartment. The search was very difficult as Joe said he could only afford $55 dollars a month for rent. We found nothing, but a few days later, Joe called me to say they were staying with a relative of Kathe's over in the East Bay town of Lafayette. I wished him and Kathe well and suggested that we stay in touch. I heard from Joe, off and on, over the next year. He called me again after a few months to say he had moved to Berkeley and that he was playing with some "far out" people he met there. Joe said he really liked Berkeley and had no desire to live in San Francisco. Joe had joined a group called the Berkeley String Quartet made up of four men who played everything from guitars, banjos, harmonica and an auto-harp to wash-tub bass, kazoo, washboard and even salad spoons.

I was really tied up at San Francisco State and delivering books to U.S. merchant ships every day, so I never made it over to Berkeley to see Joe. Sometime in 1965 Joe invited me to North Beach where he was playing—with The Berkeley String Quartet—in a coffeehouse called Coffee and Confusion. The club was on Grant Ave, and it was an old-beatnik era bar from the 50's. I took my then future wife to be Rita Milani along and we were dressed up for a night on the town, I was kind of shocked to see Joe looking like half a beatnik and half a hippie—Joe was just ahead of the fashion curve of the time so I shouldn't have been startled at all. He played the spoons, guitar, and sang that night. I was impressed that Joe was following his dream. After the gig in North Beach I tried to call him in Berkeley but the phone had been disconnected and there was no new number. I wondered if I would ever see or hear from Joe again, this time I thought for sure we were headed in totally different directions.

A few years earlier when I was in high school (1957-58) my buddies Dave Pallavicini and Noel Blincoe and I sometimes drove over to North Beach and hung out in front of Eric Nord's Bagel Shop on

Grant Ave (a well known Beat hangout of the times). We also gravi-
tated around places where live jazz was being played, being too young
to go in we would just linger out in front to hear the sounds. San Francisco was a great town to grow up in during those years. We liked to see
Eric Nord because he was like a giant, with wild hair, and a blonde
beard - sometimes he would come out in the street and talk to us. We
put on sunglasses and combed our hair funny and made the scene with
some of the beatnik's who read poetry and played bongo drums and
congas in the coffeehouses around there. It was a cool thing to do on a
Saturday night and North Beach was a happening place. One night we
saw Rock Hudson come out of the Bagel Shop, we all thought that was
really far out seeing Rock. We had no idea at the time that poets and
writers like Allen Ginsberg, Jack Kerouac, Kenneth Rexroth, Kenneth
Patchen, Michael McClure and Gary Snyder frequented those beatnik
hangouts. I clearly remember going into City Lights bookstore for the
first time then to try and buy a copy of Ginsberg's *Howl,* but it was sold
out. I had read in the San Francisco *Chronicle* that Lawrence Ferling-
hetti the owner of City Lights had been arrested for selling *Howl* so I
wanted to see what the hoopla was all about. I read it years later and
then realized why it caused such a commotion. In the early 70's Joe did
a project with Ginsberg and wrote some music for the soundtrack of a
movie Ginsberg was making called "Tricks."

In 1967 the poet Kenneth Rexroth appeared as a guest poet in one
of my Horace Mann Junior High English classes I was teaching as part
of the poets in the schools program. That same year I would see
McClure and Ginsberg at the historic Human Be-In in Golden Gate

Park. San Francisco is a big city, but at the same time it is like a small town, you keep running into the same people all the time.

We lived in the house above the La Florita House of Beauty sign – 24th St. in Noe Valley circa 1962. Photo by Ernest Cabral.

4: AND THIS IS REALLY IT

San Francisco—1967/1968

By early 1967 I was in my second year working as a classroom teacher in a San Francisco Mission District junior high school. I had just become aware of big changes going on in the Haight-Ashbury neighborhood and I was starting to develop a teaching unit on the emerging counter-culture, as it was being called, to deliver to my Social Studies class. I had no idea what was going on other than a remarkable change in how people started to look. I was very familiar with the Haight because in 1956/57 I had attended Polytechnic High School that was located only a few blocks away from Haight and Stanyon Streets.

A beginning teacher in San Francisco in 1967 started out at a salary around $6,000 per year, however rents were cheap and houses sold for under $20,000 in Daly City and around $30,000 out in the Sunset district. A young teacher could possibly qualify for a modest house. Things were rough trying to scrape by on that low salary especially with our first baby Denise on the way and the bills piling up fast. We rented a flat in the Sunset District on 44th avenue, just four blocks from the Pacific Ocean and a block away from Golden Gate Park.

I heard on the radio that a big hippie event was going to take place on Saturday, January 10th at the Polo Fields in Golden Gate Park.

Later I saw posters calling it the first annual— "Human Be-In and Gathering of the Tribes." I was really wondering about this and knew I had to be there. I called my brother Dennis Cabral, who worked as a cook and bartender in a Mission Street pool hall in Daly City, to go with me. He said that a Hell's Angel he knew named Dee had mentioned that the "Be-In" was really going to be a huge biker's convention.

On the way to the event, we encountered an endless procession of people heading into the park. I was not surprised to see what looked like thousands of mostly black Harley's parked along a dirt track. Hundreds of people came pouring in from every direction. There was a large raised stage surrounded by multi-colored banners and flags blowing hard in the afternoon wind. At the other end of the huge field, two uniformed rugby teams were fighting it out as if nothing else was going on. The rugby match added an element of surrealism to the strange event that was just getting started.

We strolled around for what seemed like hours and noticed that apparently every hippie and wanna be hippie in town was present. I kept hearing a song, by The Mojo Men that was popular at the time blaring from various portable radios, "Sit Down I Think I Love You." Some one said, "A guy named Owsley is supposed to arrive by parachute, who is Owsley?" I was not sure who Owsley was at the time. The smell of marijuana was very strong and seemed to flow over the crowd. Indian sitar music was playing on the public address system. Suddenly Jerry Garcia started playing some riffs—I think he was just tuning up - and then the Grateful Dead started to play "The Golden Road." This

Joe and Pat Kilroy of the New Age face the crowd
at the Human Be-In.
Photo by Gerhard E. Gesheidle

was the first time I saw the Dead and I was working my way close to the stage to try and take some photos to show in my class. They sounded like no band I had ever heard before.

Soon Timothy Leary started to speak about "Turning on, Tuning in and Dropping out." I was confused as to what he was really saying as I could barely hear him. There was a special feeling to all this something like the feelings a kid might get at the Circus. A local poet, Lenore Kandel, started reading love poems, then throwing the pages into the crowd. Allen Ginsberg began a chant that brought a soothing calm over the assembly. Another Al, Alan Watts gave a kind of spiritual blessing to the excited crowd. Suddenly Jerry Rubin got up and offered a brief and rambling political speech, about the Vietnam War and LBJ. While all this was going on the Hell's Angels started to surround the stage and began behaving as security forces to help keep order. The local Hell's Angel chapter president got up on stage and waved to the gathering—he got a big round of applause. The whole thing was sensory overload. I had the clear sense that I was part of and witness to some kind of important historical event that would only happen once.

When I got down to the front of the stage The Dead had just stopped playing. I looked up and saw a familiar face covered in multicolored paint. It was Joe. The last time I had seen him was in 1965 on Grant Avenue in North Beach playing in a jug band. He was just standing there on the edge of the stage, rocking back and forth holding a tambourine, staring out at the crowd. I assumed he was in the Grateful Dead—hell, I didn't know, I yelled to him, "Hey Mac, Hey Joe." I finally got his attention and he looked down at me smiled broadly and yelled back, "Wow Ron, last time we saw each other we were going in opposite directions." I really didn't know what to say except to ask him if he was part of the Grateful Dead, he said no, but that he was in a band that was soon going to play at California Hall and it was called Country Joe and The Fish. That day was the first time I heard of Joe's group. It seemed that I was learning many new things all at once.

Joe later told me a little story about what was going on in his head during the "Be-In." He said, "The main thought I had was that it was like a Viking tribal celebration and I was a Viking prince in the chief council. The medicine man was Ginsberg who led the chants and I remember Michael McClure reading a strange poem. He kept saying, over and over; and this is really it, and this is really it, and this is really it, and this is really it. During the McClure poem I was peaking on acid and thinking to myself wow—this is really it, yep this is really it all right. The whole thing was incredible and unbelievable."

"Big Daddy" Tom Donahue, who once said, "I don't trust anyone who doesn't like Country Joe."
Permission from KSAN 1971

A few months later, as summer approached, I started hearing a Country Joe and The Fish song called "Sweet Martha Lorraine" on KFRC, an AM station. It was also played heavily on the new and radical rock alternative FM San Francisco Station called KMPX and later KSAN. Famed DJ "Big Daddy" Tom Donahue led the charge by bombarding the air with the fresh and new San Francisco Sound. Donahue broke the "Summer of Love" sound out on the airwaves—Grateful Dead, Jefferson Airplane, Quicksilver Messenger Service, Steve Miller, Blue Cheer, Moby Grape, Big Brother and the Holding Company and Country Joe and The Fish. The San Francisco based groups were heard non-stop along with the Beatles, Stones, Clapton, Hendrix, and all that followed, as the "Summer of Love" was about to take off—radio never sounded better. Every time I heard Joe's tunes on the air I felt good and knew Joe was really starting to go places as an emerging rock star. I remembered what he told me three years earlier about coming to "Frisco" to break into show business. He was definitely deep into it now.

In March of '67 I saw a poster in the Haight showing Country Joe and The Fish appearing at the Avalon ballroom with the Sparrow and a group from Los Angeles called The Doors. This was to be my first visit ever to the new dance hall scene started by Chet Helms and Bill Graham. I took Rita who was 8 months pregnant, and arrived to see the line in front wrapped all the way around the block. This was the first appearance of The Doors in San Francisco and "Light My Fire" had yet to break out as a hit tune. We went to see Joe and caught The Fish set. I was a little startled when Joe sang "The-Fixin'-to-Die-Rag", it was a tune I never really listened to carefully before and it had what I thought at the time some rather chilling and sardonic lyrics—it got a real rise out of the audience.

Seeing Joe in the lobby afterwards he appeared very happy and blown away at the rocket like take off his group was experiencing. He said, "we are going on a 50-city tour, then to Europe, and to LA to make some more records and if we stay together for 20 years we will be playing jazz by then." He patted Rita on the tummy and said, "Hey let's go see The Doors." So we went in and Jim Morrison was singing "Light My Fire"—I stood transfixed under a blazing strobe light and just couldn't believe what I was seeing and hearing.

I was totally hooked by the rock'n'roll circus taking place in my hometown. By April I helped start up a rock'n'roll production company we called The Albatross. The company was made up of several investor teachers from my school, Ron Rumney, Aida Monares, and Paul Kameny plus my brother Dennis. We each chipped in a couple of hundred dollars, had 1000 posters made, advertised on **KMPX**, and rented California Hall on Polk St. The plan was to put on some good local bands, draw a big crowd and make a fortune quickly. We actually did very well considering none of us knew anything about the music business and the competition on either side of California Hall was really big—Bill Graham at the Fillmore and Chet Helms at the Avalon.

The Albatross only put on two shows, but we managed to book and present Big Brother and the Holding Company featuring Janis Joplin, Blue Cheer, and the Salvation Army Banned. This was not bad for a group of junior high teachers. I found out soon after this that Joe and Janis had been in love and living together briefly in the Haight and that Big Brother and Country Joe and The Fish often appeared together.

During the first Albatross show at California Hall held on June 29, 1967, admission was $2.50. I recall being backstage and putting several hundred dollars in $1.00 bills and quarters into a paper bag held open by Big Brother's manager Julius Karpen while the band was playing. The money came right from the front door gate receipts. Karpen at first had demanded full payment before his group would even take the stage, but relaxed when he knew we could make the $350 payment—we had given him a $350 down payment when we first booked the group a few weeks before. Big Brother and Janis had just returned to San Francisco after earning great acclaim at the Monterey Pop Festival only a week before and they were in very high spirits. In less than a year Janis Joplin would be a major rock star. None of us in Albatross knew how great Janis' performance at Monterey was, or even how important the Monterey Pop Festival was till the D.A. Pennebaker film, *Monterey Pop,* came out sometime later. Pennebaker really captured it all with close up shots of Mama Cass and Michelle Phillips of The Mama's and Papa's looking totally awe stuck, terrified and blown away while Janis electrified the audience.

We quickly found out after putting on one more Albatross show that there was no way for us schoolteacher types to compete with the Fillmore or Avalon so we soon abandoned the idea. It sure was fun, however, even if it was just for a New York minute.

Still wanting to find a way to stay involved with the music scene I started managing a series of Bay Area based rock bands. There were many new bands emerging all over and many were seeking managers. Every neighborhood seemed to have some band blasting big notes from behind garage doors. I figured since bands mainly play at night I could still teach school during the day and work with the bands in the evening hours. I started to view it as a type of part-time job. The first band I worked with briefly was called the Judge Crater Memorial Blues Band. I did manage to get them just one rather notorious gig. Before any of us knew it we were sitting on a flatbed truck in the deepest part of Hunter's Point—right in the middle of the projects. The man in charge said to me kind of jokingly, "tell your guys to play like their lives depended on it"—and they did. Then Bobby Seale took the microphone and made a rousing speech about the Black Panther party to a small crowd made up mainly of media reporters and television crews. Bobby thanked us for coming out then got in a VW Bug and drove away.

In late '67 I took on another group for about a year called Celestial Hysteria—this was a very young band which had some potential and regularly played clubs around the Bay Area like the Matrix and Dino and Carlo's in San Francisco. Celestial Hysteria has only two claims to fame. One is that they are listed in the back of a book written by the late famed critic Ralph Gleason in 1968 called *The Jefferson Airplane and the San Francisco Sound.* The other is that they played a Fillmore-West audition for Bill Graham. I decided to cease representing them right after they played at a packed teen club in San Mateo on the same bill with the emerging Santana band. Santana just a few weeks shy of releasing their first album blew them completely off the stage. I remember standing in the audience with my mouth wide open as Carlos and the boys played "Soul Sacrifice." Another more compelling reason I gave up on them was because the Hysteria members would not sign a record contract offer I had arranged for them with Sire Records. Their parents refused to give

Joe with members of Gold–1971
Photo by Ron Cabral

permission for them to sign, as they were all under 21. The parents felt strongly that the band members would have to go on tour and would soon drop out of college resulting in all of them being drafted into the Army and sent to Vietnam—as it turned out they may have been right as the Vietnam war was about to boil over. One member of Hysteria, John Barsotti, ended up taking a job at San Francisco State College and eventually became a professor in the Radio and TV Department.

In mid '68 I teamed up with my brother Dennis again, this time as co-manager of Gold, a hot and loud Mission District band that would soon have some interesting performing and recording encounters with Joe down the road. SF *Examiner* critic Phil Elwood said, "Gold had a bluesy, Airplane-Santana mix in their sound"—not a bad assessment at the time. Gold went on to play on some really big Bill Graham Fillmore and Winterland shows over the next few years. They appeared as the opening act for bands like Mike Bloomfield, Hot Tuna, Ten Years After, Big Brother and the Holding Company, Cold Blood, John Lee Hooker, and Tower of Power. Gold also landed on a bill at a San Rafael Hell's Angels party in '70 with Janis Joplin as she introduced her new Full Tilt Boogie band and said goodbye forever to Big Brother and the Holding Company. In 1971 Gold opened for Big Brother yet again at a huge anti-war march and rally that drew over 150,000 people to Golden Gate Park.

The years 1967-1973 proved to be a roller coaster ride for me in Bay Area Rock and Roll. Joe was my inspirational leader and I had the good fortune to work closely with him both at my school and during the Fillmore and Winterland gigs in '71 and '72. Joe spent countless hours working with the band as they rehearsed in a Mission District basement that was located in an alley right next to a Funeral Home. Gold also recorded a tune Joe wrote that Country Joe and The Fish had recorded earlier called "Summer Dresses." "Summer Dresses" was sung by Robin Sinclair and received lots of airplay on San Francisco radio stations.

The band also recorded part of a movie sound track for a movie Joe was in called *Que Hacer.* The film was made in Chile during 1971 and was directed by Saul Landau. Joe wrote all of the music for this unusual political bi-lingual film about the Chile of Salvador Allende. Gold continued to play "Piece of Your Action" during live performances long after recording it for the movie. Joe also appeared on a 45 record he produced for Gold under his alias Joe Borneo at Golden State Recorders. On that recording of "Summertime" Joe discreetly played keyboards. I found out later that Janis Joplin and Big Brother had recorded "Summertime" some years earlier in the same Golden State Studio.

In 1972 Joe tried an experiment and had Gold back him up on "Piece of Your Action" and "Summer Dresses" at a packed gig at Friends and Relations Hall out at the beach. That show was made up of The New Riders of the Purple Sage, Country Joe, Stoneground and Grootna. It was a gig that has never left my memory. I was extremely proud to witness my old Navy buddy Joe who had become Country Joe up there with my band playing together. It was a very sweet moment and the only time Joe ever performed "live" with Gold. During that period Joe also appeared at a few benefits for Opportunity High one being at Winterland with his All-Star band that included a former Gold conga player, the late Sebastian Nicholson. Sebastian went on to tour with Joe in Sweden and Denmark and he became a big hit over there and he ended up living in Sweden for over a year.

Joe did everything he could to help Gold succeed. They got massive exposure doing big live gigs for Bill Graham, got regular airplay and great press from the likes of John Wasserman, Phil Elwood and even Herb Caen. What kept them back was the lack of a hot LP or any LP for that matter and then the usual bickering and ego trips that almost all bands seem to go through that ultimately cause their demise. I recall the time that Fantasy Records president Saul Zaentz came over to see them personally with his wife while they were playing at Keystone Korner in San Francisco. We were told ahead of time that Saul really wanted to hear them and didn't want to be power blasted out of the club. Saul was looking for some bands to add to the Fantasy roster that might follow the path established by Creedence Clearwater Revival. Not taking all this very seriously the Gold bass player Chico Moncada, set his amp to 10, because he told us later that he liked to make the chairs rattle to get the ladies excited. Well, Zaentz and Mrs. Zaentz got up from their shimmering chairs and stormed out early in the set holding their ears. Gold had missed a golden opportunity and everything seemed to go downhill for them after that night.

By 1973 so much had happened to me since running into Joe at the "Human Be-In" five years earlier. I often remembered what Michael McClure had said it was all about... "And this is really it"... "And this is really it"...he had said, over and over. McClure was right - this was really it all right, even five years later. I was a full-time teacher, married with a growing family and house. I was also at the same time living another life in the midst of the so-called San Francisco sound explosion. I had become part of it somehow. I probably would have never even gotten involved at all if it hadn't been for Joe as I look back on it. It was only a few years before all this that Joe and I were just two young sailors in the U.S. Navy serving our country in a far off land. We never thought then about having the full catastrophe of a full time job, marriage, family, mortgage and career. By 1967 the full catastrophe had hit us both.

5: JOE AND JANIS

San Francisco -1967

Joe met Janis Joplin in early 1967 as both Country Joe and The Fish and Big Brother and the Holding Company burst onto the big time music scene. Their lives were meshed together as they found themselves caught in the musical tidal wave that peaked in the Haight that summer. Janis came out to San Francisco from Texas to break into show business just as Joe had done a few years earlier from Southern California.

Country Joe and The Fish and Big Brother and the Holding Company were two happening bands along with the Grateful Dead, Jefferson Airplane and Quicksilver Messenger Service. Joe and Janis often were billed together at the Fillmore and Avalon ballrooms during the early days of the San Francisco music explosion in the late 60's.

Joe rarely spoke of his relationship with Janis. "It was just a very normal love affair between two people who shared exciting times in the Haight," he often said.

Whenever Joe could be prodded into talking about her, it became obvious that he, to this day, has very strong feelings for her. "The first time I saw Janis was in early 1967 at a gig in San Francisco when Chet Helms introduced her on stage as a friend from Texas.

We played a gig together right after her San Francisco gig in Berkeley at the Golden Sheaf Bakery. I was on acid. My little brother Billy was there."

After the Golden Sheaf, Janis and Joe just got together. As their personal relationship developed, their bands played the same show at the Avalon. "Soon I started spending nights with her at a flat she shared in San Francisco," said Joe. "Later I moved in with her for a while when she got her own place—actually I didn't have anyplace to live at the time."

Joe and Janis had a brief and very normal boy friend-girl friend thing—that's about it. They lived together for about three months and they became good friends. They experienced all the activities going on in the Haight-Ashbury. The couple seemed a good fit for each other, but like so many things in Janis' life, she burned with incredible intensity that may have proven to be too all consuming for Joe and they soon broke up.

Joe maintained that the real reason for the break up was the constant interference from both of their careers. Joe said, "I was never comfortable living in San Francisco. I considered Berkeley to be my town so I moved back—it was as simple as that."

Joe later ran into Janis from time to time at various concerts. At Woodstock Janis had been doing heroin, and her set with Kozmic

Blues Band sounded somewhat disjointed. The set was filmed for inclusion in the Woodstock movie but never made the final cut. I am convinced if Janis had appeared with Big Brother and the Holding Company she would have been the star of both the festival and the subsequent movie. Janis brought a crowd of 10,000 to their feet two years earlier performing with Big Brother and the Holding Company at the Monterey Pop Festival and she could have done it again at Woodstock.

Janis
Photo by Steve Brown.

Albatross Productions Poster from June 29, 1967 California Hall,
SanFrancisco
Artist Gut. From Ron Cabral collection.

♦

I first met Janis on the 29th of June of 1967 after I hired Big Brother to play at California Hall for Albatross Productions. Albatross Productions was made up of myself, my brother Dennis and some teachers from my school. We thought we could make a make a buck off the hard-core San Francisco music scene. One of the reasons such a rag tag group like Albatross was able to get Big Brother was because Rodney Albin, a friend and fellow San Francisco teacher, had put in a good word to his brother Peter Albin who just happened to be the bass player in Big Brother.

Our gig was scheduled to go on ten days after the Monterey Pop Festival that had made a serious career breakthrough happen for both Big Brother and the Holding Company and Country Joe and The Fish. The Festival also showcased acts like Jimi Hendrix, The Who, and Otis Redding. We had no idea at the time what had just taken place in Monterey. It cost us the Albatross $750 to book Big Brother before the Monterey Pop Festival for one 45-minute set. By 1969, around the time of Woodstock, Janis was pulling down $50,000 per show and Country Joe and The Fish commanded $10,000.

ED Denson (he spells his first name ED), Joe's former manager told me, "The Fish needed to charge that much (in 1969) because we were about to go to war with China, and all American political subversives were going to be purged and put in jail." Denson said, "We thought we needed to make a lot of money before that happened." I think Denson was putting me on as the war with China never did happen, but he made me think about it.

We expected a full house for the Big Brother show at California Hall, but only about 500 people showed up for the Thursday night presentation—lots of competition existed from The Fillmore and Family Dog and too bad for us it wasn't held on a Friday night. We were disappointed because we had made and distributed 1000 posters all over the Bay Area and we had advertised on radio KMPX. Milan Melvin a radio personality on KMPX was the emcee. Milan was upset, he said, "I expected to see the line wrapped around the block—Don't they know what just happened in Monterey?" I shrugged my shoulders, as I had no idea what he was talking about. When Janis arrived she was by herself and dressed all in black. She did not go the dressing room, but hung out by the concession stand eating chips and drinking beer while checking out the small crowd. I experienced some weird sensations when I introduced myself to her and thanked her for appearing at the opening Albatross gig. She just looked at me, smiled and nodded her head.

We had hired a poster artist called Gut who charged us $200 to make a poster that would eventually become a collector's item. Turns out Gut was also a Hell's Angel and manager of Blue Cheer. Seems Gut may have been a bit ripped when he was working and misspelled Big Brother spelling it "Big Broter." Dave Pallavicini made the second Albatross poster for the 4th of July show featuring Blue Cheer and the New Salvation Army Banned. It was a red, white and blue poster with a guy looking like Uncle Sam in the middle pointing out with the typical "I WANT YOU" pose.

Aside from the lack of any profit on the show, we were all excited when Big Brother finally took the stage. The band played a series of thundering tunes right from the yet to be released LP *Cheap Thrills.* Just back from Monterey Pop they were primed and pumped up. Janis and the band tore the place up with "Piece of My Heart" then "Down on Me" driving our small audience crazy. When the set ended the foot stomping from the crowd brought Big Brother out again and they did an encore of "Piece of My Heart."

The next time I saw Janis was three years later in 1970 at an annual Hell's Angels' party. It was held in San Rafael across the Golden Gate Bridge in Marin. The place was called Pepperland (formerly the Citadel); it was basically a ballroom that was attached to a motel. It had a capacity of about 2,000 that soon filled up with wall-to-wall people.

I was there as the manager of my band Gold that really lucked out getting on this huge bill. The lineup was Janis Joplin headlining with Big Brother and Full Tilt Boogie. Third bill was Gold, and Loose Gravel was the opening act.

At the time I was a 28-year-old Dean of Boy's working at Presidio Junior High in the Richmond District of San Francisco. I was excited about this event and met the band members at Pepperland after driving over there directly after work. When I arrived I stashed my tie and sport coat in the trunk of the car and put on my cowboy hat. It was surreal seeing the marquee listing Janis/Big Brother, Main Squeeze and Gold. Loose Gravel was not listed. The marquee had mistakenly listed Main Squeeze, a band she had briefly experimented with next to Big Brother when it should have said Full Tilt Boogie, but Janis wanted to surprise everyone.

Hells Angel's Party in San Rafael Poster—1970
Hells Angels is a registed trademark of Hells Angels Motorcyle Corporation.
Courtesy of HAMC.

Big Brother and The Holding Company after Janis left the group. L to R James Gurley, Peter Albin, Sam Andrew, Dave Getz
Courtesy Sam Andrew collection, ED Denson collection and the Mike Somavilla collection.

I went straight to the backstage dressing room. I had an incredible rush when I saw that we were in the same room with all the Big Brother members: Peter Albin, Sam Andrew, James Gurley, Dave Getz and Janis. Film star Michael J. Pollard (Bonnie and Clyde) was there and big time record producer Albert Grossman from LA was there. I also saw members of Full Tilt Boogie, a band that Janis had hand picked herself to record the yet to be released *Pearl* LP. The tension between the new and old bands was astounding. This gig was historic because it was to be the last time Janis would ever perform with Big Brother, and it was her first ever-public appearance with Full Tilt.

Soon a huge buffalo sized Hell's Angel, the backstage manager, came in the room and blurted out, "Hey Gold, get your asses on stage you have one minute." I walked out to the floor to get a handle on what was going on. Loose Gravel, a serious biker band, was finishing up their set with the heaviest riffs I had ever heard at that point in my life—or at least it seemed that way. Loose Gravel, was led by Mike Wilhelm who I recognized as a former member of The Charlatans. They were red hot and shooting steam. I saw one Angel, with a far away look in his eyes, cracking a long black bullwhip for no apparent reason— CRAAAAAAAAAAAK. Then another Angel appeared from across the room and he was also cracking a whip. The crowd just made space for them to crack those whips. I quickly went back to the band room again, lit a Kool and tried to look cool, calm and collected. I tried to tell Dennis about the guys with the whips but he just stared straight ahead with big eyes and said nothing. A few hours earlier I had been holding detention at the school—I kept thinking about school.

Moose, yet another massively sized Hell's Angel and the San Francisco chapter president, came back to reassure us that everything was just fine. Gold had gotten this gig because Moose often came to see the band play at Keystone Korner in North Beach, and he really liked the band. He was also a friend of my co-manager and brother Dennis. Moose had a hand in getting Gold an earlier gig with Malo and Hot Tuna at Longshoreman's Hall the year before at a benefit for a clap clinic sponsored by the San Francisco Hell's Angels.

"Follow me, lets go—it's Showtime boys", the backstage manager yelled. Joe Bajza, the lead guitarist of Gold, chugged down what was left of his Colt 45 beer; he then strung his telecaster over his shoulder and headed for the door. Richard Coco, the lead singer, cinched up his tight fitting leather pants and left the room with bass player Chico Moncada, drummer Louis Goursau and conga player Sebastian Nicholson.

Showtime took on a whole new meaning. Redheaded Ed Scott, rhythm guitar player for Gold, was determined but seemed a little shaky and pale as he pointed at with me his Gibson guitar. "Hey man, I ain't going out there unless you come with me."

I had no choice but to go, because my options were to stay in a room full of Hell's Angels, or to join an audience filled with hordes of Angels and some of them cracking bullwhips. As we walked into the jammed packed dance floor towards the stage I noticed a large sign that said, "Check Guns Here." I suddenly realized that I had to go to work at the school the next day. I was in charge of discipline. I don't know why I remembered that; it just came into my mind for no apparent reason. When we got to the stage it was packed solid with all the equipment of the four bands playing. I positioned myself on top of a speaker amplifier just slightly behind a curtain, and I had the best seat in the house for the show that unfolded during the next three hours.

Gold played like they were possessed and they were very well received. During the last Gold tune "Season of the Witch" Janis and Big Brother appeared back stage. Gold had played a very loud and powerful set—they had to. Just as they were leaving the stage Janis yelled to Coco who was holding a cowbell to stay put. She shouted, "Hey man, play some Latin on that cowbell will ya."

From the Ron Cabral collection
GOLD - L TO R: Sebastian Nicholson, Bob Golden,
Joe Bajza, Louis Goursau, Robin Sinclair, Chico Moncada and Ed Scott.

Richard Coco 1970 - lead singer of Gold danced on stage with Janis at the Hell's Angels party.
Photo Coutesy of Ed Scott Collection

Well what could Coco do?—He played some Latin. Soon Janis and Coco were dancing all over the stage bumping asses in the process while Peter Albin started to lay down those wavery and wicked Big Brother bass riffs. During the first number a naked woman, jumped up on stage and started dancing around; then a naked man appeared out of nowhere, he jumped on top of her and all eyes shifted to them. Janis and Peter Albin went over to them and just stopped and looked. The man suddenly got up and jumped off the stage; then Janis gently told her to get off the stage. The woman quickly jumped back into the audience and started dancing by herself, seemingly oblivious to the thousands of Hell's Angels all around her. Strange things always happen at Hell's Angels parties. I observed that there were other naked people in the audience but no one seemed to notice. The smell of weed suddenly became overpowering.

Big Brother then stepped up for what would be their final public set with Janis. Janis had a crew of women back stage who attended her during the set like handmaidens to a queen. After each tune or during a long James Gurley solo, Janis would skirt behind an amplifier and take big gulps from a bottle of whiskey handed to her by one of her girls while others wiped the sweat off her brow. She polished off an entire bottle of Southern Comfort and smoked several cigarettes during the set, and it didn't seem to faze her a bit. She seemed totally focused. The band concluded with Janis wailing on "Down on Me" to the roars of the frenzied and totally stoned Angels. Janis always put on an extremely high energy and vigorous performance that you had to see to believe.

Finally, the highlight of the evening began with Janis introducing the members of her new band Full Tilt Boogie. John Till, Richard Bell, Ken Pearson, Clark Pearson, and Brad Campbell all stepped out. "Sometimes I call them "Pearl Bailey," she said. The audience went wild in Pepperland as the band played every tune from the forthcoming "Pearl" album note for note.

As the grand finale came, and the set ended, Janis simply passed out and fell hard over Gold's drum set knocking them all over the stage—she appeared to be out cold. Some have said a Hell's Angel hit her over the head with a beer bottle, but I did not see that. A cymbal landed out in the crowd. Suddenly three very muscular Hell's Angels jumped up on stage and picked up her limp body high over their heads as if she were a wounded Viking. Janis' head was back and she was slack jawed. One of the Angels grabbed the microphone and bellowed, "All right you fuckers, let's hear it for Janis Joplin." When Janis awoke backstage she asked some people in the room if she had done ok with the performance then she started crying because she couldn't remember what happened. She did a lot better than ok, she knocked the audience out—tough to do at an Angels party.

They had carried her off the stage while the huge crowd thundered applause yelling and screaming Janis, Janis, and Janis over and over. The screaming and yelling for Janis went on for a long time. She had given what may have been her greatest performance ever even surpassing her awesome performance in the Monterey Pop movie. The gig was finally over; I was completely dumfounded by the spectacle and totally speechless.

Janis was found dead in a hotel room a few months after the Hell's Angels party. She was only 27—apparently the drugs and the booze had just killed her. Throughout her intense substance abuse, her raw talent was always obvious. Many of the musicians at that time had a serious run in with the drug scene and it led to the demise of many of them.

Joe knew about drugs too but he avoided heroin and the life-style he viewed that was associated with it. He said, "The Monterey Pop Festival in '67 was the peak of my psychedelic period. I took STP the day before we played, and I was really stoned out. Monterey Pop was the end of childhood for a lot of Bay Area bands. After Monterey, the big time record industry really hit San Francisco. The music scene made the cover of Time magazine and the whole business became commercial."

Joe said, "Two years after the Monterey Pop Festival, Janis performed at Woodstock. I thought she was trying too hard. She made the same mistake The Fish had made earlier when we played exhausted. I have this lingering memory of Janis at Woodstock. She looked bad, she was unhealthy looking and she was just plain angry. When Janis was together, she was really nice, but when she got junked she could be not so nice to be around. Janis could be a regular person whenever she felt like it. She was friendly but had a quick temper that got her into a lot of fights. She was ambitious, loved her career, and loved her dog George; she was a great singer and performer and I miss her."

Joe wrote a song for her called Janis that he still performs to this day.

JANIS

words and music by Joe McDonald

Copyright © 1967 by Joyful Wisdom Music BMI

Into my life on waves of electrical sound
and flashing light she came
into my life with the twist of a dial
the wave of her hand the warmth of her smile
and even though I know that you and I
could never find the kind of love we wanted
together alone—I find myself missing you
—and I—you and I.
It's not very often that something special happens
and you happen to be that something special for me
walking on grass where we rolled and laughed in the moonlight
I find myself thinking of you
—and I—you and I—you and I.

Into my eye comes visions of patterns
designs the image of her I see
into my mind the smell of her hair
the sound of her voice—we once were there
and even though I know that you and I
could never find the kind of love we wanted
together alone I find myself missing you
—and I—you and I—you.

Janis back stage
Photo by Steve Brown.

6: COUNTRY JOE AND THE FISH

Country Joe and The Fish formed in Berkeley in 1965. Eugene "ED" Denson, the group's first manager, made up the name Country Joe and The Fish. Because Joe was the only member of the band named Joe, everyone started calling him Country Joe. It seemed fitting because, after all, Joe's parents named him after Stalin who was known as "Country Joe" during World War II. The "Fish" came from a Chairman Mao quote that Denson found in a book, "The fish who swim in the sea of the people."

The band was started as just Joe and his friend Barry Melton who played lead guitar. The group was first known as

Joe and Barry as the Frozen Jug Band—
Photo by Gene Anthony

Original packaging
of Rag Baby

the Instant Action Jug Band, before the name was changed. Throughout the life of the band, many members came and went, but Joe and Barry were constant. Keyboarder David Cohen, Gary "Chicken" Hirsh, the drummer, and Bruce Barthol on bass were all longtime members and contributors to the band. Several other musicians including Dave Getz, Peter Albin, Mark Kapner, Doug Metzner and Greg Dewey played off and on with Joe and Barry as members of The Fish.

As was true for many bands, the late 60's proved to be a golden age for Country Joe and The Fish.

The anti-war movement was really heating up as Country Joe and The Fish played their first gigs around the Bay Area.

Joe, Denson, and Mike Beardslee published *Rag Baby,* a little magazine out of Berkeley. On one issue Joe failed to produce enough copy, so he and Denson decided to put out a "talking issue" with his anti-Vietnam war protest tune on it. "We went over to Chris Strachwitz' house and recorded it. We pressed it on a 33 & 1/3rd record, a new format at the time, and then we sold it at a teach-in against the war in Vietnam at the UC Berkeley Campus," said Joe. Denson said, "We were "uniting the folk scene" and presenting new songs like "Fire in the City". Joe and I produced the two EP's. The first was sold in the magazine and the second was issued on its own. By that time the band and the record were more important than the magazine."

L to R: Barry Melton, David Cohen, Bruce Barthol, Country Joe, "Chicken" Gary Hirsh. The "classic" Country Joe and The Fish—photo by Jim Marshall

Country Joe and The Fish Poster from a 1967 gig in Vancouver, Canada. Artist Bob Masse. Courtesy of Bob Masse collection.

In 1967 Country Joe and The Fish had been signed by Vanguard Records and soon recorded "*Electric Music For the Mind and Body*" which was one of the first "psychedelic" records.

Denson said, "At the time the two big Bay Area venues were the Avalon Ballroom, run by Chet Helms, and the Fillmore with Bill Graham. The Avalon was hipper, the Fillmore paid better. Country Joe and The Fish were a bit marginal at both. We didn't quite have the commercial edge of the Jefferson Airplane, which gave Bill some qualms about hiring us often, and Helms felt that our politics were not hippie enough. Or perhaps it is better to say that having politics wasn't hippie. I do recall negotiating a record contract in the upstairs lobby of the Avalon while on acid, which seemed pretty hippie to me. The contract fell through however."

When the Vanguard LP was finally ready for release Denson talked them into doing a release party at the Fillmore. The label hired the hall and booked Big Brother and the Holding Company and another band to play. They invited all the industry people, record store buyers and members of the media to come. Then they printed up invitation cards and handed them out in the Haight-Ashbury. Thousands of people showed up—way too many to get into the hall. This event was a very big success and really put the band on the map. Denson said, "This showed that lots of people really wanted to hear the band's music."

By 1967 and 1968 Country Joe and The Fish was playing regularly at Fillmore West in San Francisco and Fillmore East in New York City. Thousands of rock'n'roll fans stood in long lines to get into the shows. Serious psychedelic fans timed their Saturday night acid trip to peak during The Fish set. In the early days, Country Joe and The Fish head-lined over some newcomers and relative unknowns like the new group Led Zeppelin.

Not So Sweet Martha Lorraine

words and music by Joe McDonald
© 1967 Joyful Wisdom Music BMI

She hides in an attic concealed on a shelf

Top billing for Country Joe and The Fish

Behind volumes of literature based on herself

And runs across the pages like some tiny elf

Knowing that it's hard to find

Stuff way back in her mind,

Winds up spending all of her time

Trying to memorize every line,

Sweet Lorraine, ah, Sweet Lorraine.

Sweet lady of death wants me to die

So she can come sit by my bedside and sigh

And wipe away the tears from all my friends eyes

Then softly she will explain

Just exactly who was to blame

For causing me to go insane

And finally blow out my brain,

Sweet Lorraine, ah, Sweet Lorraine.

Well you know that it's a shame and a pity

You were raised up in the city

And you never learned nothing 'bout country ways,

Ah, 'bout country ways.

The joy of life she dresses in black

With celestial secrets engraved in her back

And her face keeps flashing that she's got The Knack,

But you know when you look into her eyes

All she's learned she's had to memorize

And the only way you'll ever get her high

Is to let her do her thing and then watch you die,

Sweet Lorraine, ah, Sweet Lorraine.

Now she's the one who gives us all those magical things

And reads us stories out of the I Ching,

Then she passes out a whole new basket of rings

That when you put on your hand

Makes you one of the Angel Band

And gives you the power to be a man,

But what it does for her you never quite understand

Sweet Lorraine, ah, Sweet Lorraine.

Well you know that it's a shame and a pity

You were raised up in the city

And you never learned nothing 'bout country ways,

Oh 'bout country ways, oh 'bout country ways,

Yeah, about country ways, oh, country ways...

Joe wrote the song "I-Feel-Like-I'm-Fixin'-to-Die Rag" in the summer of 1965. He was living in a flat with his first wife Kathe. "We had just come up to the Bay Area a few months before from Southern California. One day, a woman named Nina Serrano came to my place and asked me to write music for an anti-Vietnam war play opening at the UC Berkeley and San Francisco State campuses," Joe said. "I started working right away and wrote 'Who am I' in three days."

Who Am I?

words and music by Joe McDonald
© 1967 Joyful Wisdom Music BMI

Who am I
To stand and wonder, to wait
While the wheels of fate
Slowly grind my life away.
Who am I?
There were some things that I loved one time,
But the dreams are gone I thought were mine,
And the hidden tears that once could fall
Now burn inside at the thought of all
The years of waste, the years of crime
Passions of a heart so blind;
To think that, but even still

As I stand exposed, the feelings are felt
And I cry into the echo of my loneliness.
Who am I
To stand and wonder, to wait
While the wheels of fate
Slowly grind my life away.
Who am I?
What a nothing I've made of life
The empty words, the coward's plight
To be pushed and passed from hand to hand
Never daring to speak, never daring to stand
And the emptiness of my family's eyes
Reminds me over and over of lies
And promises and deeds undone
And now again I want to run
But now there is nowhere to run to.
Who am I
To stand and wonder, to wait
While the wheels of fate
Slowly grind my life away.
Who am I?
And now my friend we meet again
We shall see which one will bend
Under the strain of death's golden eyes
Which one of us shall win the prize
To live and which one will die

'Tis I, my friend, yes 'tis I
Shall kill to live again and again
To clutch the throat of sweet revenge
For life is here only for the taking.
Who am I
To stand and wonder, to wait
While the wheels of fate
Slowly grind my life away.
Who am I? Who am I?

"After I finished the last verse to 'Who Am I,' I sat back in my chair relaxing and strummed some chords. "I started writing 1-2-3 what are we fighting for? and so on, and in about 30 minutes, I finished the song—the melody and lyrics just seemed to flow out of me." A Vietnam vet named Richard Hughes provides this memory he has of hearing the "Fixin to Die Rag" while he was in Vietnam. "During the war the Army used to have psych-ops helo's. They would fly out at night and drop flyers and broadcast propaganda over VC positions. These things were noisy! They could be heard for miles—loud speakers on the order of 40,000 watts. When returning back over American positions they sometimes changed the record on more than one occasion I heard the "Viet Nam Rag" from those loudspeakers perhaps a mile away." James Sterba writing about Marines in Vietnam for the New York Times on July 14,1969 said, "The lack of revelry here is most apparent at night. From inside the dusty tents comes quiet talk. There is no frolicking, and except for a few morbid jokes, little humor. Artillery guns boom *explosives out of the camp throughout the night disturbing precious sleep. From a tape recorder in one bunker, came psychedelic sound seemingly more appropriate to Greenwich Village that to Vandergrift Combat Base: And its one, two, three, what are we fighting for? Don't ask me I don't give a damn, next stop is Vietnam...The song by the rock'n'roll group called Country Joe and The Fish is popular here. The only way to keep from blowing your mind here is to joke about death, said a member of the First Battalion. The nickname of the battalion is the Walking Dead. "Worrying about dying is how guys get killed out here," said another.*

Ron Cabral

I-Feel-Like-I'm-Fixin'-To-Die Rag

words and music by Joe McDonald

Yeah, come on all of you, big strong men,

Uncle Sam needs your help again.

He's got himself in a terrible jam

Way down yonder in Vietnam

So put down your books and pick up a gun,

We're gonna have a whole lotta fun.

And it's one, two, three,

What are we fighting for?

Don't ask me, I don't give a damn,

Next stop is Vietnam;

And it's five, six, seven,

Open up the pearly gates,

Well there ain't no time to wonder why,

Whoopee! we're all gonna die.

Well, come on generals, let's move fast;

Your big chance has come at last.

Gotta go out and get those reds—

The only good commie is the one who's dead

And you know that peace can only be won

When we've blown 'em all to kingdom come.

And it's one, two, three,

What are we fighting for?

Don't ask me, I don't give a damn,

Next stop is Vietnam;

And it's five, six, seven,

Open up the pearly gates,

Well there ain't no time to wonder why

Whoopee! we're all gonna die.

Huh!

Well, come on Wall Street, don't move slow,

Why man, this is war au-go-go.

There's plenty good money to be made

By supplying the Army with the tools of the trade,

Just hope and pray that if they drop the bomb,

They drop it on the Viet Cong.

And it's one, two, three,

What are we fighting for?

Don't ask me, I don't give a damn,

Next stop is Vietnam.

And it's five, six, seven,

Open up the pearly gates,

Well there ain't no time to wonder why

whoopee! we're all gonna die.

Well, come on mothers throughout the land,

Pack your boys off to Vietnam.

Come on fathers, don't hesitate,

Send 'em off before it's too late.

Be the first one on your block

To have your boy come home in a box.

And it's one, two, three

What are we fighting for?

Don't ask me, I don't give a damn,

Next stop is Vietnam.

And it's five, six, seven,

Open up the pearly gates,

Well there ain't no time to wonder why,

whoopee! we're all gonna die.

The late days of the 60's were the most frantic for The Fish. I went to a 1968 Bill Graham Fillmore concert in San Francisco that head-lined Country Joe and The Fish, Steppenwolf and a local band called The Flamin' Groovies. The hall was packed like sardines and the smell of weed and incense was unmistakable. Giant red and black balloons were flying all over the ballroom. A paisley patterned light show was shimmering on the wall behind the stage—a kind of pulsating purple glow appeared on and off. A topless woman in a long hippie style skirt took up a strategic position right in front of the massive public address system. Someone threw a large bouquet of flowers on to the stage. I was totally stoned from the dope smoke, and the whole scene was freaky—surreal.

Steppenwolf in a wild fury shook the house. John Kay and his group were riding high on their smash hits "Born to be Wild" and "Magic Carpet Ride," and they kicked ass. Soon it was time for the headliner to appear. Country Joe and The Fish attacked the stage at midnight to a heavy surge of audience energy. Joe grabbed the microphone cord and swung it around like a soul singer. Chicken Hirsh laid down a steady and soul-style drum beat, then Barry Melton stepped forward and belted out in his raspy voice, "we want to dedicate this song to L.B.J." The band broke out into Super bird, and the audience went crazy.

Ron Cabral

Superbird

words and music by Joe McDonald

Well, look up yonder in the sky what is that I pray?

Yeah, it's a bird, it's a plane, it's a man insane,

It's my president, whew, L.B.J.

I said he's flyin' high way up in the sky just like Superman,

But I got a little piece of kryptonite,

I'm gonna, whew, bring him back to land.

I said come out Lyndon with your hands held high,

Drop your guns, baby, reach for the sky.

I got you surrounded and you ain't got a chance,

Send you back to Texas, make you work on your ranch,

Yeah, yeah.

Well, he can call Super Woman and his Super Dogs,

But it won't do him no good,

Yeah, I found out why from a Russian spy

He ain't nothin' but a comic book.

We're gonna pull him off the stands and clean up the land,

We're gonna start us a brand new day.

And what is more I got the Fantastic Four

And Spiderman to help him on his way.

I said come out Lyndon with your hands held high,

Drop your guns, baby, reach for the sky.

I got you surrounded and you ain't got a chance,

Gonna send you back to Texas, make you work on your ranch,

Yeah, yeah.

Yeah, we're gonna make him an agricultural worker...

Part of his own poverty program.

The next song Joe dedicated to Mr. James Brown. With "Rock and Soul", Joe tried to prove that rock music has soul too if you can "dig it."

Rock and Soul Music

words and music by Bruce Barthol, David Cohen, Gary Hirsh, Barry Melton and Joe McDonald
© 1968 by Joyful Wisdom BMI

Hmm...

We'd like to take this opportunity now to play you a little thing that we learned from Mr. James Brown the King of soul music. Now this ain't soul music, mind you, this is rock music. But it's got soul to it, if you can dig that. And now the band would like to play a new riff they just learned, we call a sockin'-it-to-you riff. And it-uh goes something like this.

Alright; are you ready boys?

Let me hear you do it one time just once c'mon

Huh! Ah that's it, do it again!

Huh! Oh come on!

Oh it feels so good, do it again!

Alright, come on! Huh!

One more time, come on! Huh!

Now let me hear you do it two times if you can. Huh huh!

Alright, that's good, do it again! Huh uh.

Hmm alright, come on. Huh.

Oh yeah, do it again now. Huh uh.

Feels so good, once more! Huh uh.

Oh let me hear you do it three times now, huh!

Ah yeah, come on!

Alright! Four times now!

Ahhhh! come on now.

Oh, when you hold me, ah

Oh, when you kiss me

Oh, when you love me

It's alright, outasite,

Ahhh! you know that you're just d-d-d-d-d-dynamite!

Huh!

I guess you've heard all about rock and roll,

You've heard about the music that they call soul.

Well, I'm here to tell you what I've been told

'Bout the brand new music called the rock & soul.

Rock & soul yeah, that's the music got you walkin' down the street

Clappin' your hands, kickin' your feet, (Rock & soul)

Jumpin' up and down oh it's so groovy, oh rock & soul, yeah.

Now everywhere I go, you know that it's always understood

Rock and soul music is doggone good.

Now everywhere I go, from Kansas City up to Maine

Rock and soul music's driving people insane.

Rock & soul, yes it's the music got you walkin' down the street

Clappin' your hands, kickin' your feet, (Oh rock & soul)

Jumpin' up and down, oh, it's so groovy, rock & soul, rock on, yeah, huh!

Ha!

Now everywhere I go you know that it's always understood,

Rock and soul music is doggone good.

Now everywhere I go, from Kansas City up to Maine

Rock and soul music's driving people insane.

Rock & soul, yeah it's the music got you walkin' down the street

Clappin' your hands, kickin' your feet, (Rock & soul)

Jumpin' up and down, oh, you're gonna be so outasite, rock & soul yeah.

Oh, you know we're al-almost, almost through.

You just gotta get one, one, one more little thing together here before we go.

Play your bass, son, c'mon, ah yeah c'mon, do it, ha!

Sock it to me

Sock it to me

Sock it to me.

Ah! your love is like a rainbow

I said, ha, ah your love is like a rainbow darling

You know your love is like a rainbow

I say hey your love is like a rainbow

Oh falling all around my shoulders

Falling all around my shoulders,

You know that your uh love is like a rainbow

Now falling all around my shoulders, yeah, and I

Love you, you know I do, alright, huh.

The band's frantic energy climaxed as the audience sang along with Joe the lyrics of "I-Feel-Like-I'm-Fixin'-To-Die Rag." On my way out the door I overheard three very drunk Marines in uniform discussing the show they had just witnessed.

"I thought there was suppose to be a dance here with some girls," said a big-ass shorthaired Marine. In various degrees of shock, they stumbled back onto Fillmore Street looking for action.

The next time I saw Country Joe and The Fish perform was in 1969 on the David Frost TV Show. The band played "Fixin'-To-Die" during prime time to a national audience. A week later, Frost got a sack full of letters condemning him for having a "sick, unpatriotic" act on his show. Frost passed the letters to Joe.

"December 20, 1969

Dear Mr. Frost:

It has taken me a week to compose myself after seeing your show with "Country Joe and The Fish". Did you stop to think that in your home audience there might have been some mothers that lost sons in Viet Nam? "Be the first one on your block to have your boy come home in a box." We here in the West know how bad the S.D.S is. Is someone putting the pressure on you to expose left-wing extremists? You actually smiled and applauded those creatures when they finished. The housewives doing their ironing in the late afternoon like to laugh and see pleasant things. You Mr. Frost are a bitter disappointment.

Mrs. W.A.

Concord, California"

"December 17, 1969

As a member of the silent majority, I was offended by the David Frost Show. It reached a new low in bad taste. How any network could permit that "kettle of Fish" with their anti-American song and their unsightly garments to go before the American public is incredible. It was the ultimate ugliness to say the least. Mr. Agnew was right about the mass media. The whole show was a Frost.

L.L.D.

NY, NY"

December 12, 1969

"Mr. Frost,

The unbathed folk group who sang about Vietnam this morning should be shipped to any country of their choice. They are cowards of the worst degree. I'm proud to say my son fought and met the commies standing for freedom. He was shot 3 times. CBS should pay the folk singers to leave the country.

Mrs. S.D.
Provo, Utah"

December 12, 1969

"Dear Mr. Frost,

After seeing those things "The Fish" I felt like going to the bathroom and throwing up. Your show has hit rock bottom and you have just lost this viewer.

Mr. & Mrs. R.F.B.
Van Nuys, California"

December 12, 1969

Sirs:

Shame—the dirty unkempt creeps (The Fish) and their song on Viet Nan were disgraceful. The weak audience applauded. We tuned you out for good.—TRASH—SCUM

A former listener

The Commonwealth Motel, Boston, Massachusetts"

December 6, 1969

"Mr. Frost,

I must protest vehemently your presentation of the obnoxious singing group called "Country Joe and The Fish" singing that repugnant song concerning the war in Viet Nam. The lyrics appalled me especially the line: "be the first one on your block to have your boy come home in a box". In behalf of every mother whose son died in Viet Nam I am asking you in all humanity not to present these dirty unwashed people to us again with all their verbal diarrhea spewing from their filthy minds and mouths. I refuse to patronize any of the sponsors if this situation ever occurs again.

M.K.P.

Carbondale, Pennsylvania"

December 5, 1969

Gentlemen,

Last night, December 4, 1969, the show was excellent except for the last few minutes. Why-oh-why did the beautiful interview with the Robb's have to be debased by a hoarse voiced, hairy unwashed creature giving forth with what I assumed was supposed to be a song? I thought it was a most unfortunate finale to one of the otherwise best shows you have ever done.

E.L.A

Bowie, Maryland

"Dear David Frost,

We both have great respect for your show and watch it daily. We considered it great and high class. However today after Linda Bird and Charles Robb—how dare you give us that bearded slob who looks like a Tate murderer!!!! He sang like an animal in pain!!!! If you omit his kind, be assured your rating will not go down!!

Sincerely,

Mr. And Mrs. H.H.

North Miami Beach, Florida"

December 10, 1969

"Dear Sirs: I would like to register my disgust and horror at the number I am watching at present on the **DAVID FROST SHOW**, Wednesday December 10th—the combo is called Country Joe and The Fish and the song "What are we fighting for?" at the dinner hour no less, when children are watching, it is blasphemous, disrespectful and anti-everything decent. I am not for War but this is too much.

Mr. G.B.

Cleveland, Ohio"

December 10, 1969

"Mr. Frost,

I am really disgusted with you for permitting that disgraceful song to be sung by those unkempt men or are they really women. I'm only 21 but these men embarrass me with their horrible appearance and shocking lyrics.

Yours Truly

Mrs. F.C.

Bellerose, New York"

Joe on stage at Woodstock getting ready
to go on solo—photo by Jim Marshall

Joe always felt that his song was misunderstood. The letter writers and thousands of others didn't realize that the song they hated so badly really attempted to address the horror of war with dark sarcastic humor known by soldiers everywhere as "GI Humor."

GI humor is a way people have of bitching in a way that will not get them in trouble, and that also keeps them from insanity that can be experienced during war. Today America has a volunteer military, but during the Vietnam War, many people joined because they thought it was the right thing to do. It was patriotic. But, far more people were drafted. A great number of others in trouble with the law were given a choice of going into the military or going to jail. It was kind of government blackmail. Many chose to leave the USA and head for places like Canada.

During the war some people were drafted into the Marine Corps, which was one service that seldom drafted (it did during the end of WWII especially after losing so many men at Iwo Jima). Few people realized that the casualty rate for Marines was actually higher in Vietnam than in World War II. As it turned out over 58,000 American GI's never came back home from a war we ended up pulling out from and losing.

Country Joe and The Fish had been booked to appear on the Ed Sullivan show earlier in the year in 1969, but their appearance was suddenly cancelled even though they were paid in advance. They did appear on Johnny Carson and Joe appeared on Hugh Hefner's "Playboy after Dark" a very popular late night TV show.

On the Hefner show it concluded with Joe singing the lyrics to "Fixin'-To-Die" while plastic go-go dancers boogied up a storm. This was another very bizarre display of 60's weirdness as expressed in the media.

1969 was a big year for Country Joe and The Fish. At Woodstock they were added to the program at the last minute, it was a toss up between them and Jethro Tull, and The Fish got the nod as Tull wanted to be paid big bucks in front. The Fish do not appear listed on the official poster.

"We got $2500 bucks, and I flew out a day early 'cause I wanted to watch the show, said Joe. I checked into The Holiday Inn near the site that was packed with show people including Janis Joplin. Janis invited me up to her room. It was like old times, we just talked and had a good time. Then she broke out a needle and started shooting up. I hated that shit so I got really pissed and just left."

Janis was upset at Joe's reaction, and tried to talk Joe into staying, but Janis' was just too bad off. "I had talked to her girl friend Peggy on the plane out, and I was unhappy to learn that Janis was back on heroin," said Joe. After leaving Janis, Joe went out to try and get on the chopper to go to the site. He found out that it would not take off as it was unsafe to fly after dark. So Joe stayed in his room that night.

The next day Denson arrived with the band. He said, "When we got to the hotel it was so crowded that we couldn't get a room until someone left. Arlo Guthrie was in the room we were to get and we had to wait in the hall until he left. The transportation to the site was in collapse. The band and I went by car and it took hours. We had to drive right through the crowd, with people walking along in front of the car. We had to ask people to move out of the way so we could inch forward."

The first day of the show, Joe did not ride with Denson and the band but hitched a ride with a worker who drove him right up there to the stage area.

"I went up on the stage and saw all those people, and almost freaked," said Joe. "I sat down and watched Richie Havens sing."

After Richie was finished singing, Bill Belmont and John Morris the Emcee came over and asked Joe to go out and sing solo. Joe didn't have his guitar, so Morris got one, and they put a rope around it for a strap and pushed Joe out to the front of the stage.

"I started to sing something and no one was paying any attention, so I walked off the stage and asked Belmont if I could do "The F Cheer," said Joe. Belmont said to go for it. "No one is paying attention anyway," so Joe walked back out there and yelled, "Gimme an F."

The entire crowd stopped talking, looked up at Joe and yelled "U." It just accelerated from there. After the "F" Cheer Joe went right into "I-Feel-Like-I'm-Fixin'-to-Die" Rag. According to Joe, "I didn't know they were filming me." Joe was the only performer to sing twice—once solo and once with the band. A few months later Joe saw the footage and was "blown away."

"When we recorded the "I-Feel-Like-Fixin'-To-Die Rag" for Vanguard Records, I decided to put the "F Cheer" at the front of the song. We actually spelled out FISH, but in the summer of '69 at the Shaefer Beer Festival in New York City we said, "let's change The Fish cheer to The Fuck cheer." Joe said, "So The Fuck cheer was born, and the people loved it—so we just kept it in the act. The only problem was, the Shaefer Beer people banned us from future beer fests, and the band was cancelled from a scheduled appearance on the Ed Sullivan Show. We figured fuck 'em if they can't take a joke," said Joe.

I was able to catch up with both Barry Melton and David Cohen who have fond, but often sordid, memories of the Fish days.

Barry said, "I remember our first Country Joe and The Fish tour the best. Joe and me as a duo, touring Northwest Colleges. The Students for a Democratic Society (SDS) sponsored the first tour. We had a lot of fun on that tour. As I get older I remember the good times." Joe said, "Barry was 18 at the time and I was 23 and Barry could score weed in any town in a matter of minutes." Joe went on, "Once up in Oregon at Reed College we took some acid and went out into the forest. Barry fell over a log and into a creek. We started laughing till we had tears in our eyes, then we started talking to the little forest people who lived under the rocks."

"People think that playing in a band is glamorous," said Cohen. "But, when someone asks me about it, I usually say we were on the plane, then in a car, then in a hotel room, then the car, then the airplane...and on and on. But, it was tremendous fun, and I loved it."

To sum up David's view on the subject, "the music made it all worthwhile," he said.

The Fish formed by accident. "We just sort of were in the same place at the same time," Barry said. "The first time we played together was at the 1965 Berkeley Folk Festival. We were on the steps of the Student Union, playing with other musicians who typically gathered on the periphery of folk festivals of the early 60's." Barry said, "Of the first two songs recorded by Country Joe and The Fish one variation featured Joe and me on "Superbird" and the other featured Joe, me, Bob Steel, Cavel Bass, Carl Schrager, and Mike Beardslee on "Fixin-to-Die Rag." Our first amplified gig featured me on electric and acoustic guitar, Richard Saunders on bass and Joe on acoustic guitar. Richard stopped playing with us around the time we started playing electric music."

The group went on to the Monterey Pop Festival and Woodstock.

The Monterey Pop movie was shot on a shoestring. But, that Festival contained the hope, promise and idealism of the era. Two years later, by the time of the Woodstock movie, much of what went wrong with the Sixties became obvious.

Both David and Barry wrote for The Fish. Barry wrote, "Sing, Sing, Sing", "The Love Machine" and "Doctor of Electricity". David wrote most of "Rock and Soul Music", "Thursday" and "Eastern Jam". "Ninety-nine percent of the really good songs were written by Joe," said David.

The end of the sixties marked the end for the most part of Country Joe and The Fish. The breakup came in 1970, about the time the Woodstock movie came out.

At the time of Woodstock, The Fish was touring extensively with "sidemen" Mark Kapner on Keyboards, Doug Meltzer on bass and Greg Dewey on drums. The band was successful with the *CJ Fish* LP, and the movie starring Don Johnson, *Zachariah,* featuring Joe and the Fish as a band of outlaws, was released. Even this success wasn't enough.

Left, Monterey Pop Revisited poster. Top right, panel discussion with Bruce Barthol, Barry Melton, and Jorma Kaukonen. Bottom right, Country Joe, David Cohen, Mark Naftalin, and Bruce Barthol. Photos by Ron Cabral. Poster Courtesy of Tom Wilkes

David Cohen and Joe as a duo in 2000.
Photo by Todd Bolton

David felt that the band broke up partly because they were no longer playing the really beautiful pieces that Joe wrote. "Instead, we played extended jams loosely based on some of the songs, and the music had degenerated to a point that I was no longer enjoying playing it much myself."

David still gigs regularly in New York and with Joe on occasion. In November of 2000 they performed together on the East Coast and in Washington State. Cohen is still close to Bruce Barthol and he talks to "Chicken" Hirsh once in a while. Barry continues to perform as Barry "The Fish" Melton with musicians like Peter Albin and communicates regularly with "ED" Denson and Bill Belmont who was the road manager during the glory years.

Joe tried to reform the old band several times but it never happened. Barry and David are both skeptical about the band ever reforming. There have been several versions of Country Joe and The Fish that have evolved, even one version without Joe called The Psychedelic Fish that toured very briefly after Joe left in 1970.

A reunion attempt made in 1994 at the Fillmore in San Francisco ended up in shambles. The gig was highly advertised and was well attended as many fans of Country Joe and The Fish came out hoping to see a great show. What actually happened was that Barry refused to play with Joe and the group. He came out first and did a 20-minute solo acoustic set walked off and left the building. The Friday before the gig Barry passed out literature saying he was not allowed to play at the reunion - it is unclear why Barry did this. Joe and the band did their set without Barry. This disaster of a gig really upset the Bill Graham Presents staff and totally soured Joe on trying to do another reunion.

David Cohen said, "The closest we came to actually reforming was in December of 2000 when Joe, me and "Chicken" were suppose to play together in Seattle with the Bevis Frond band. At the last minute "Chicken" just chickened out." Joe and David went on as a duo and both had fun so much in fact that they continue to appear from time to time as the Dynamic Duo around the country. David gets part of the credit for making Country Joe and The Fish the historic psychedelic band it became—his performance on "*Electric Music for the Mind and Body*" speaks for itself. His haunting organ and keyboard playing together with Barry's lead guitar really created a most unusual sound.

In June of 2001 Joe, David, Bruce Barthol, and Barry Melton found themselves all together at a three-day nostalgic event in Monterey called "Monterey Pop Revisited." The History and Arts Commission of Monterey put on the event. The History and Arts people maintained that the Monterey Pop Festival was a historic event that needed to be acknowledged as such. Not only did 50,000 wild hippies flock peacefully to the quiet town of Monterey in 1967 but also, it was a rare and highly eclectic music festival unseen before this time. Putting Ravi Shankar on the same bill with the Mama's and the Papa's was just unheard of outside of Bill Graham's selections for his shows at the Fillmore.

Joe, David and former Butterfield/ Bloomfield/Electric Flag keyboardist Mark Naftalin played the opening night party on June 15, 2001 at the Monterey Maritime Museum that featured a photo and art display of highlights from the 1967 Festival. Joe wore a white helmet like he did in 1967 and played some classic FISH tunes like: "Section 43", "Porpoise Mouth", "Sweet Martha Lorraine", "Janis", "Who am I", and "Fixin'- to- Die- Rag."

Monterey Pop helped launch the careers of Jimi Hendrix, Janis Joplin, The Who, Otis Redding, Jefferson Airplane and Country Joe and The Fish. The Monterey Pop movie says it all and it was shown during the weekend. The 75-year-old filmmaker D.A. Pennebaker was there to explain how he made the film and why he stressed the incredible performances of Ravi Shankar, Country Joe and The Fish and Janis in the film.

The next night Barry, Bruce and David played together at a Monterey club on Cannery Row called Sly McFly's. On Sunday Joe joined Barry and David who played at the Monterey Fairgrounds along with

Mark Naftalin. Joining them were Roy Blumenfeld and Andy Kulberg from The Blues Project. The weekend turned out to be a sort of Country Joe and The Fish weekend in Monterey. This was the first time in years that so many original Country Joe and The Fish members were together in one place.

Is there a chance for a real Country Joe and The Fish reunion someday? Well it almost happened in Monterey, not so long ago, and of course anything is possible. With many groups from the 60's reforming and touring in 2003 like Big Brother and the Holding Company, Canned Heat, It's A Beautiful Day, Iron Butterfly, Hot Tuna (Jorma Kaukonen and Jack Casady), Sons of Champlin, Strawberry Alarm Clock, Steve Miller to name just a few - some great concerts could be on the horizon. All of these musicians from the old groups that are re-forming for that one last tour are all well over 50 and many at or near 60. How long can they keep playing? Who knows? To some seeing the old musicians back on stage would be like seeing baseball stars like Yogi Berra or Willie Mays back in the line up with the Yankees and Giants...It would be great to see them play again but we would be horrified at what the reality would be. Maybe that is why Grace Slick retired. Maybe she could have hung in for a little longer. Carlos Santana is not slowing down with age he seems to be getting better.

Musicians can play well into there 80's. In the summer of 2000 I saw Les Paul who is over 80 performing with his trio at the Iridium in New York City. Les could still make "Maria Elena" sound heavenly on his guitar. He did say during the breaks that he had to go downstairs and take a little nap. He would disappear for a while and come back up and continue to play. Look at all the terrific Jazz and Dixieland musicians in New Orleans who are way past retirement age and they can still wail. Picture Ringo Starr, Mick Jagger, Bob Dylan, Carlos Santana, David Bowie, Paul McCartney, Neil Young, Jorma Kaukonen, and Country Joe at 70 or older. Will they still be making music? My guess is yes and they will all probably make the cover of *Modern Maturity.*

Despite an early end to the band Country Joe and The Fish, Joe continues to perform as Country Joe, and Barry as Barry "The Fish" Melton. Finding himself without a band Joe began his solo career in 1970. He founded another band briefly in 1972 called The All-Star Band, but soon after a highly expensive European tour that almost caused a bankruptcy he disbanded it and went on to refine his solo career. The All-Star Band did manage to record the highly acclaimed LP "*Paris Sessions*" before breaking up.

Joe has reunited with Barry on occasion as Country Joe and The Fish even as late as the early 1990's. Country Joe and The Fish were always just Joe and Barry and whoever else they wanted to have in the band. Barry once suggested to Joe that maybe they could drag out the Country Joe and The Fish bit from time to time for ceremonial events and for mutually agreeable charitable causes. Joe has however, managed to survive as a solo and recording artist for over 30 years no matter what has happened to Country Joe and The Fish. Joe recorded an LP called *Eat Flowers and Kiss Babies* with a band from Europe called Bevis Frond that can recreate the sound of early Country Joe and The Fish. Barry plays in clubs regularly mainly in Northern California and can also be found practicing law at the Yolo County Public Defender's

Office in Woodland, California. "ED" Denson the original manager of Country Joe and The Fish has also passed the Bar and practices in rural Northern California.

Will Country Joe and The Fish reform in some form if they are ever inducted into the Rock and Roll Hall of Fame? Count on it. Maybe then it will happen.

Barry "The Fish" Melton in 1974. Barry founded Country Joe and The Fish with Joe McDonald in 1965. Photo Courtesy of Barry Melton.

Bruce Barthol and David Cohen in 2001. Photo by Todd Bolton.
Bruce is a Producer of the San Francisco Mine Troupe.
David gigs heavily on the East Coast.

7: ROCKING EDUCATION

San Francisco

Country Joe and The Fish went on to great success during the period 1967–1970. Their critically acclaimed performances at Monterey Pop, Fillmore West and East, the Avalon, in Europe and the huge climax at Woodstock in 1969 were the highpoints of a surging roller coaster ride. Several more albums were released during this period and the "Fish Cheer" and the "Fixin'-to-Die Rag" were now engrained in every Country Joe and the Fish performance. Millions around the world heard these tunes while following the bouncing ball in the Woodstock movie. "Fixin'-to-Die Rag" became the low moan that turned in to a high wail against the war in Vietnam. But as all things must pass, The Fish were starting to have ego trip problems and were soon to break up. Joe began a new career as a solo artist.

It was now 1969 and I was assigned to a new alternative high school called simply Opportunity High. It was established for so-called disenfranchised youth and was located in an old storefront in the South of Market area. The district was known as SOMA or South of Market—another way of saying on the other side of the tracks.

I had been able to keep my day job, work with bands, and was able to take care of my growing family. The band Gold was set up in our garage in a very straight neighborhood on a steep hill in Daly City.

From the living room window there was a glorious view of the Pacific when it was visible. Most of the time, however, we were just fogged in and could not see across the street. The band operated out of there until 1973—rehearsing and doing a string of regular gigs all over the Bay Area, Northern California and Oregon. Our neighbors were good about not complaining about the comings and goings at all hours of these long haired musicians, or the bass and guitar amplifiers often on volume 10 regularly pouring out big sounds from behind that blue garage door—I think they actually enjoyed it. The bands greatest hope at this time was to get a chance to play at Bill Graham's Fillmore West.

Rolling Stone magazine, whose office headquarters was only a few blocks away from the school on 3rd Street, sent a young reporter named Amy Hill over to do a story on alternative education and interview some of the students who were in my Urban Studies class.

Soon after that I called *Rolling Stone* to see if we could take some kids over there on a field trip. Ben Fong-Torres called me back and said to bring them over. When we arrived at *Rolling Stone's* offices Ben met us at the door. He then led a tour around the spaces introducing us to various writers and staff members while playing with a yo-yo.

It was around this time that I invited Joe to come over and give a talk about whatever he wanted to for the small 150-member student body. Joe agreed to come and when he arrived the students were already gathered in an assembly area. I introduced Joe to the students and staff as my old Navy buddy and welcomed him to the school. Joe had just gotten back from a trip to London and Germany and he was beat. He started to speak about the war in Vietnam and the Black Panthers. One kid blurted out, "Hey man I though you were going to play some tunes." Most of the students just stared at Joe in disbelief that a star of Woodstock would take time out to come and be with them at their school—most of the kids knew him from the movie *Woodstock* and from the LP which had long ago turned "Gold." Most of them also had seen Country Joe and The Fish play at one time or another around the area. Joe made a lot of new friends that day.

Afterwards as we stood on the sidewalk on Mission Street, he told me he would like to come back someday and maybe be a volunteer teacher. He said he would like to teach some classes like song writing, recording, and possibly even a class on the music business. I told him that sounded great and to let me know when he was ready to do this. I was very excited about Joe's interest in doing this and knew how lucky his future students would be to have him as a teacher.

Ironically Joe and his wife Robin Menken had just been featured on the cover of Rolling Stone. This cover came out right after his appearance at the school. The Opportunity students were highly sophisticated when it came to music, as many of them regularly attended the major rock shows put on at the Fillmore and the Avalon. They raved about bands like: Led Zeppelin, Cream, Hendrix, The Stones, Traffic, Deep Purple, Steve Wonder, Ike and Tina Turner, Chuck Berry, Jefferson Airplane, Janis Joplin, Procol Harem, Moody Blues, Crosby, Stills, Nash and Young, Creedence Clearwater, the Kinks, Alice Cooper, Frank Zappa, Jeff Beck, Traffic, Chicago, Pink Floyd, Dave Mason, The Band, Santana, and the Grateful Dead. These kids had seen the best of the best and on a regular basis.

Bill Graham now had the lead in promoting and was already being referred to in the media as the "Rock Czar." Graham really knew how to put great shows together and he did that time and time again. In just a few short years he became the greatest promoter of rock'n'roll in the world. He would soon open up Winterland, an ancient ice-skating arena, near the old Fillmore auditorium, as an additional venue. He also started booking acts into the Cow Palace, Candlestick Park, the Oakland Coliseum, The Greek Theatre in Berkeley, Concord Pavilion, Shoreline Pavilion, The San Francisco Civic Auditorium (which was later named after Bill after he died in a terrible helicopter crash in 1991) and other venues. At the same time he was doing the same thing on the East Coast especially in New York and in Europe. When he had time he worked as an actor appearing in several major movies, like *Apocalypse Now* with Martin Sheen and Marlon Brando and *Gardens of Stone* with James Caan.

Graham had also been holding auditions for new talent for some time on Monday nights at the Fillmore West on Market Street. Admission was $1.00 and three bands would play a 45-minute set. Graham and his staff would pick any standouts and offer them a third bill slot for union scale on a show with major established groups. The selected band would be advertised in the media and get their name included on a Fillmore Poster. Celestial Hysteria late in their career, and Gold early in the game, got a chance to play at these audition nights. Gold went on to appear on several major Bill Graham Presents shows with groups like: Ten Years After, Big Brother and the Holding Company, Mike

Bloomfield, Bola Sete, Chicago Slim, Hot Tuna, Cold Blood, Joy of Cooking and Tower of Power to name a few.

I did not see Joe again until late 1971. He had gone solo and was on a heavy road schedule as well as recording and working on new songs. I was now on the pilot faculty at the newest San Francisco alternative high school called Opportunity 2 High—note the 2. The school had broken away from the old Opportunity High which was much more conservative. The old Opportunity later became known as Downtown High and found a home inside an old Ford factory in the Mission district.

The new Opportunity 2 High was housed in a South of Market location, this time an old warehouse at 739 Bryant Street one block from the San Francisco police headquarters and the Hall of Justice. Staff was selected for their creative qualities and strong teaching styles. No one was directly assigned, but had to volunteer for duty at this particular school. Likewise students had to apply and go through an interview process before they could enroll.

The students were drawn from four groups: 16 year olds who did not complete junior high school. Unwed mothers who did not wish to return to neighborhood schools. 18 to 21 year olds who did not complete high school for reasons like chronic truancy, social and academic failure. Dropouts who wished a final chance to earn a GED or diploma. During the interview students were set straight on what was expected of them and they had to sit in a room with all 12 teachers present.

The school was to house no more than 150 students. Classes would be very small and each teacher also had to act as a counselor for 15 students. There was no official principal as the staff elected a teacher to be the head teacher on a rotating basis. There was no authoritarian atmosphere. The entire building was covered with student art, posters of every description, and fresh paint. The curriculum was standard, but hyphenated as in English/poetry, PE/tai chi, PE/karate, civics/Vietnam War studies, biology/sex education, science/bird watching, biology/fishing, music/rock and roll and jazz, music/street musicianship, music/guitar lessons, art/photography and video. There were also classes in basic reading and practical math as well as community service and GED preparations. Field trips were taken regularly to locations all over California. The school ran like a tight jam session.

Prior to the Opportunity schools in San Francisco students not making it in the big comprehensive high schools were sent to so-called Continuation high schools. Continuation schools were for the most part bleak and dreary places and many of the students would simply drop out. Conditions in these holding centers were archaic, repressive, and they were run like junior prisons. There was no joy or passion for learning in the Continuation schools.

The idea for Opportunity High came in 1968 from a group of young radical and progressive educators trained at UC Berkeley. Several of the founders led by teachers Marcia Perlstein and Judy Bebelaar conceived a plan for a new approach on how to deal with turned off students. During the late 60's the San Francisco School District desperately needed such a plan since they were feeling the impact of what the

Haight-Ashbury scene had done to school attendance. It was a time of "turn-on and drop-out"—a time of anti-war and peace marches and far out people in the streets. It was a time when new and powerful drugs of all types had hit epic proportions and became available in every neighborhood of the city.

Ken Dondero, a former shop teacher and sailboat mechanic, called us together and told us that the new Superintendent of Schools, Dr. Tom Shaheen wanted to meet with us. Dondero had arranged the meeting for a Saturday to take place in his backyard over in Marin County. Nothing like this had ever happened to us before so we were all curious about what Shaheen had to say. Shaheen had just recently been appointed to be the new Superintendent and had come to San Francisco directly from Rockford, Illinois. He came right to the point, "Do whatever it takes to reach the kids assigned to your school—you must reach them, there is no one else to do it. You have my direct order to do this." That was all we needed to hear, we knew we had support at the top. That meeting with the Superintendent really set the tone for what was to take place at the school over the next few years.

After the meeting with Shaheen I called Joe that day and asked him if he would like to teach a class or two if we could arrange it. I was totally surprised when he said yes and that he had some available time to start right away. Joe came over to the school the next week driving a large motorcycle. First I took Joe from class to class and introduced him to the teachers and students. After school, a meeting of the staff was held to meet with Joe to plan a teaching schedule with him. Joe was considered a volunteer teacher and professional consultant. Most of the teachers knew of Joe as the leader of Country Joe and The Fish and were amazed that he was about to join the staff. There were a few other people in this category teaching poetry, art and martial arts. Prior to the staff meeting numerous students came in to see Joe and to tell him they would sign up for one of his classes. Joe was told he would have to es-

tablish a plan for his curriculum and grading expectations. He would be required to advertise the classes, noting the time the class met and the room location.

Concert flyer

The next day Joe was back with his plan ready to implement. He told Marcia Perlstein, the head teacher that he was going to teach three music electives and they were General Song Writing, Women's Song Writing, and LP Record Production. He started putting up flyers on the walls of the school announcing these new classes and soon he had more students than he could handle. All the teachers started telling their students to take a class from Country Joe. Everyone soon noticed Joe's presence in the school. I was very pleased that Joe was doing this, as I knew his efforts would greatly influence many students in a most positive and special way.

Joe teaching his song writing class at Opportunity High School 1972.
Photo by Judy Bebelaar.

My classroom was downstairs and it was really just a little addition put together with 2 by 4's and plywood. It was used mainly as a place for the school rock band to practice in. There was a set of drums and a piano in the room. Once in a while Joe would come down there and give some guitar lessons mainly to my classroom assistant Ed Dee and a few students. Ed was teaching guitar to at least 12 students every day. Ed also was sitting in on Joe's song writing class. The school hired former Lemon Piper, Mike Perroti, a drummer with Gold, to teach percussion. On occasion some members of Gold like Robin Sinclair, guitarist Ed Scott and percussionist Percy "Sebastian" Nicholson came by the school to jam with students. Robin was an outstanding vocalist who prior to joining Gold had recorded two albums for Cadet Concept a branch of Chess Records. The musical atmosphere around the school was really starting to pick up.

Besides Ed Dee, there were several very good student guitar players enrolled in Opportunity High. One was a student named Abel Zarate who I met at the old Opportunity High on Mission St., he later played guitar in a band called Malo. Malo was George Santana's band, and he is the brother of Carlos Santana. Malo went on to have some top 40 hits, "Suavecito" being one. Once Joe Bajza the lead guitar player of Gold came to the school and jammed a little with Zarate. Bajza was very amazed and somewhat blown away that a high school kid could play so well. Another student guitar player was Robert Graves, a totally awesome lead guitarist. Graves had a gigantic professional sound and had very advanced technique—I never knew what became of him.

Once before, Zarate had asked my brother Dennis and me if we would manage a band he was with then called Brown Sugar. Well, we were not really interested in managing that band but felt that maybe we could get them a gig or two to play with Gold. After about a week Abel and his drummer came over the house unexpectedly and told us they needed $5,000.00 in a hurry to buy some new equipment. It seemed that the garage they used on Florida Street had been broken into and all their equipment had been stolen. Needless to say we had to terminate our very brief relationship. I think Zarate went on to have a fairly successful career in music.

After six months of teaching at the school some members of the School Newspaper, asked Joe for an interview. Joe agreed and here is some of that interview.

An Interview with Country Joe
By Jeff Gardipee and Mary Robertson
October 1972

Q. As a volunteer teacher working with students here at Opportunity what do you see happening with the students that are in your classes?

A. It changed me to have a dialog with them and it changed them to have a dialog with me. I enjoy seeing a student use me in a clear rational way to get whatever help or knowledge he or she needs in order to get to the needed place. I am there to help the student go somewhere.

Q. What has the interaction at the school done to your self-concept?

A. As a teacher you can't keep what you have to your self. One of the objectives towards becoming a good teacher should not be to have students idolize you. The main objective should be to get it out what ever you have to give them and then give it to them. You have to be selfless in order to do that. I have become more aware as I see more of what I have to do. For instance when I first started I thought I could just come on my schedule and give some classes, but then I began to see that if really wanted to get more done I would have to come down to the school on a regular basis. I would have to discipline myself by arriving at the times I said I would be there. That is kind of a selfless act just showing up on time.

Q. What is the main role of a teacher as you see it?

A. I think that in most regular schools teachers are an end in themselves. The schools are set up to give grades and the grades become an end in themselves. I see the staff at this school working like a real team. The teacher is one vehicle operating with a team of other vehicles that make up the faculty. Some teachers can be very free and others rigid and structured. It takes all kinds to make up a team. I have seen that every teacher in this school agrees that they are there to help the student go out there and function in the real world. I see that students here are learning things they can apply to their daily lives. I like the idea that learning is valued more than earning grades.

Q. What are your thoughts on the grading system: A, B, C, D, and F?

A. Gimme an F, no just joking. The A, B, C, thing might be ok for some people but what about the kid who gets all D's or worse yet all F's. Getting all F's for whatever reason could be a serious blow to that student's permanent self-image. When he or she looks in the mirror and thinks, hey I got all F's that must mean I am a complete and total failure—rough thing to happen to a kid of say 16. Maybe the teachers ought to look at how they grade. In my Music class I gave high grades to people who made music. This was the first semester I was asked to give grades and credits. I have made it a rule to give passing grades to those who make music all the time. However I realize that a person who earns an A is no better or no smarter than someone who earns a C.

Q. Do you think there is a drug problem in this school?

A. Well, no but some people in the school may have such a problem. Just a year ago one of the teacher aides Miriam Geli who I knew, died from what I was told was an overdose of a downer drug called Reds or Seconal. I have a copy of DOPE NOTES a little book that was published a few months ago about what some students here at this very school have to say about their drug experiences—it is very revealing. Herb Caen was so taken by DOPE NOTES that he wrote an entire column in the Chronicle about it. Losing Miriam was terrible for everyone and I attended the funeral along with some students and staff it was a very sad day. Maybe one thing the schools can do is having better relations with drug clinics like the Haight-Ashbury medical center. They could have counselors on call to help students who are referred or who need special help. You know public schools could do a better job if they helped the kid who has it so bad at home that it gets in the way of any learning. What I am trying to say is a student comes to school bummed out because his father or mother was bummed out and they screamed at him or worse. So the kid starts taking drugs. The teacher and counselor and dean could stand on their head to help the kid, but he has to go back to that bad trip at home. He doesn't want to go home but he doesn't have any money and he has no job. His parents probably wouldn't mind if he ran away, they probably don't want him around anyway. Maybe public schools should have full-blown boarding schools for the neglected and unloved kid. Maybe that would help ease a heck of a lot of pain.

Q. Is there any message you would like to tell young teachers just starting out?

A. I would tell them to get their "chops up".

Q. What do you mean by "chops up"

A. "Chops up" is a musicians term meaning to make every note count and to cut out any unnecessary **BS**. Try to remain open, positive and friendly. Having your act together is important, because in performing if your act is sloppy and is not together you will lose your audience. Teaching and performing have a lot in common. In a musical sense when a musician or group of musicians have their "chops up", that means when they go on stage they can play with the concepts originally developed and they can play well. When the "chops are down" nothing works right. In the classroom be prepared at all times and know were you are going. Be aware that you have the power to push open space.

Q. How long will you stay with us at Opportunity High?

A. Not sure really, maybe another year or so. I am very committed to doing this and I really enjoy everything about being here. My songwriting and recording classes are coming along really well and I want to start a music business class next semester with the possible help of some people I know. I will be taking a new band out on the road soon so I will have to miss some months here and there.

Q. What is the name of your new band?

A. I am calling it Country Joe and The All-Stars and there are several members in it that have played in some really well known bands from around here.

Q. Can you say who the well-known band members are?

A. No it is kind of a secret for the moment.

Q. Thank you for the interview and good luck

A. Thanks I enjoyed it.

8: MANDRAKE'S

Berkeley - 1972

As Joe was leaving his class at Opportunity for the weekend he mentioned that he was trying out some new horn players for his, brand new, band he called Country Joe and The All-Stars. They were about to play a four nightstand at a well-known club in Berkeley called Mandrake's. I asked him if he was trying out any trombone players and he said no because he hadn't run across any. Well at that point I told him I knew one—me. Joe looked at me with an amused look on his face and just said, "yeah, be there in two hours for a rehearsal and don't be late."

For some time I had been playing my trombone around school mainly with jazz teacher Bob Morrow and some jazz players he would bring in. Sometimes I would play on occasion with Gold just for fun. I started playing when I was in the 7th grade band and just kept right on playing it. My tone was good and I could still hit a high C. I could still double and triple tongue - so I figured I might do ok. As a kid I took private lessons from Phil Laspina, the first chair trombonist of the San Francisco symphony. Then later with Gary Drumm a big band player who had once played with the Tommy Dorsey band. I had also played in the City College of San Francisco jazz band and the San Francisco State concert orchestra once during a summer session. I knew I would have to play very well, as Joe was a very accomplished trombone player

127

and he would not stand for any clunker notes. I remembered the time I heard Joe play once in Japan when he sat in with a Japanese dance band doing Glenn Miller tunes. He played better than any of the professional trombonists in that band—he had a very polished tone and he was very good with the high and low ranges.

I was very excited that this was happening. I asked students Jeff Gardipee, Ted Strong, and Fred Wagner to go with me for moral support and to consider it a field trip on how to audition for a band. We ran out to the car and raced out onto the freeway straight to Daly City to pick up my ancient "Olds" trombone. It was the same trombone I played in my high school band and the same one I took to Japan and used at the jam sessions with Joe in 1960.

Sebastian went from Gold to The All-Star band in 1972. Photo by
Ron Cabral.

Arriving at Mandrake's, in a downpour, we spent what seemed like 20 minutes getting soaked and pounding on the back door. Then Peter Albin who I knew as the bass player for Big Brother and the Holding Company finally opened the door and let us in. I was now getting extreme butterflies and weak knees. The stage at Mandrake's was loaded with equipment and there were about a dozen musicians milling around. A four-man video crew was also setting up. Soon Joe came busting into the room and said, "ok, let's do it." Suddenly I saw a smiling Sebastian Nicholson walking up to a set of congas—he winked at me. I was confused, Sebastian was Gold's conga player, I wondered what was he doing up there—he never told me he was playing in Joe's band. Joe came over and said, "I like that kid and I might take him on the road with us, now get your trombone ready we are running out of time here." I went behind the stage and tried to warm up by blowing some pedal notes (deep low notes below the scale). I then added some Sure-slick (lubrication fluid) to the slide then walked out on the stage past the drummer I recognized as Dave Getz also from Big Brother and the Holding Company.

Joe and Tucky Bailey at Mandrake's in Berkeley 1972. Photo by Ron Cabral.

Joe introduced me to the trumpet player he was trying out, a guy named Steve Carvalho, and to the sax and flute player Tucky Bailey. He also introduced me to Dorothy Moscowitz who played outstanding keyboards. "Any charts", I asked? Steve said, "Huh, no charts ya just got to play, and try and fill any holes, just follow some of my patterns." Now my heart was really pounding, neither Steve nor I had ever heard this particular band play before and we were talking about filling holes. I knew I would have to play like never before, just let it come out. Sometimes jazz and rock musicians, poets, painters and other artists experience a sort of strange and mystical energy that enters their body during a performance and very creative things start to happen - must be the phenomena called The Muse. I was hoping The Muse would guide me and maybe hop on my shoulder for at least the next four nights. I thought back to the time I met a monster guitar player (I think it was Howard Leese) at the 1970 Vortex festival at Oregon's McIver State Park near Portland. He was playing an incredible, huge, Jimi Hendrix on acid like solo during a (PA) - public address system check. Impressed at how well he played I asked him point blank how he did that. He said, "Well I just feel something in me and my entire body seem to know what to do. I am not aware that I am controlling my hands or fingers, sometimes I actually am not even aware of my body at all while playing—it is like I have become a marionette and someone is pulling the strings."

Joe passed out the order of tunes and said, "let's go through the entire set non-stop—one and two and hit it." Then all eleven musicians came to life as one and the set was on. Fortunately for me I had heard most of Joe's tunes before and I had a pretty good ear. At first it was a very strange feeling for me to be on that stage, but as we went through each tune it felt better and better. At times I lost the key but my good ear helped me out. Some of the tunes played that night were: "Fantasy", "Sweet Lorraine", "Guantanamera", "Fixin'-to-Die Rag"— Dixieland style, "Janis", "On the Road Again", "Hold on It's Coming", and some Bill Withers tunes like "Use Me Up." At 9:00 p.m. the set was repeated as the four-hour performance was set to start then. At 1:00 a.m. Joe came over to Steve and I and said, "Ok, can you guys come back tomorrow night and do this again?" I could not believe this whole thing had taken place—I thought I was dreaming, but I wasn't.

Famous jazz singer and San Francisco *Chronicle* music critic Jon Hendricks wrote a review on the Mandrake's gig. Here are some brief excerpts from the review.

Country Joe's Got a Brand New Band

Holding it all together was Country Joe, guitarist, vocalist, schoolteacher, recording artist, music historian, scat singer (yes I said scat), bon vivant, composer, lyricist, entertainer, and pop star whenever he feels like it.

Yeah it's all coming together, folks—Joe has the respect for the blues I'm so aware of lately. In fact, he's teaching it at Opportunity High School No. 2 in San Francisco. His range of historical knowledge is deep and abiding and it is my pleasure to meet him and listen to him talk about what we all love—the blues.

Yes, there will be a revival of at least bigger bands, if not big bands and Joe It is nice to see the future look so rosy. Joe McDonald, Country Joe McDonald if you please, will be right there in the vanguard of it.

Ron Cabral played trombone but did not solo he also played percussion.

Copyright Chronicle Publishing Co. 1972

Well I played the entire 4-night stand and will always regard it as the highlight of my personal trombone playing, thanks to Joe. I often thought about this and realized I had played in a band with members of Big Brother and the Holding Company and Country Joe and The Fish. It was like if I had been given a chance to play in four games on a big league baseball team with some major league all-stars. It was as if I was trapped inside a fantasy, but it wasn't a fantasy at all. Later on during my long career with the San Francisco Schools I would often play trombone or drums at assemblies with ad hoc bands created for the faculty talent shows at various schools I worked at. Playing with the All-Stars was a great confidence builder.

The All-Star band went on the road right after Mandrake's playing all over the U.S. and then France, Denmark, Norway and Sweden. The album *Paris Sessions* was recorded at this time. By late 1973 the group had become a quartet and was back in Berkeley playing at Mandrake's again. Peter Albin was still in the group on bass, as was Dorothy Moscowitz on keyboards and a new member Ginny Walker on drums. I went over to see them and noticed that the four of them took up the entire stage. I wondered how eleven of us fit up on the stage just a few months back on that same stage.

Not everything was as rosy as Jon Hendricks had predicted, however, for Joe and The All- Star's. The band cost Joe a huge fortune to take on the road during the year and finances were at an all time low. Soon Joe would have to fire everyone connected with the All-Stars and go solo again. There would be some very hard times ahead.

The All-Star Band: L to R - Peter Albin, Tucky Bailey, Country Joe, Dorothy Moscowitz, and Ginny Walker - Photo by Paul Kagen. From the Joe McDonald collection

9: SUMMERLAND

Bimbo's 365 Club—North Beach

San Francisco - 1973

Joe was getting near the end of his year and a half stint as a volunteer teacher at Opportunity High. He needed to shift his attention back full time on his music career, but he wanted to leave the students with something memorable and exciting. He decided to offer one final class called The Music Business in Theory and Practice. To start the class, he invited none other than Bill Graham to the school to give a talk on the nature of the music business, as only he knew it. Bill knew about Joe's work at Opportunity, and he readily agreed to appear.

Graham's visit excited most everyone at the school. When he finally arrived a sort of pandemonium broke loose with the students. Many could not believe he would come - but there he was. They all knew Bill as they had seen him handing out apples at the top of the stairs at the Fillmore. Chairs were set up on the ground floor of the school and soon all of them were full. Graham spoke without a microphone and all could easily hear his booming voice.

He spoke at length about his previous work with the San Francisco Mime Troupe, and the development of the rock and roll ballroom and concert scene in the Bay Area. He gave his formula for box office success and that translated into one word, "draw." He stated that well-known groups with hot records on the market draw lots of people willing to buy an album and a ticket. Unknown groups with no records on the market draw flies.

Bill knew what he was talking about. He constantly put together shows so artistically solid that he was in a class by himself. His sense of drama, broad knowledge of the music, and his highly aggressive business drive made him the best in the business.

However, his ego was fueled by his terrific success, and he was known as quite a son of a bitch. He demonstrated his true nature on his frequent tirades at band managers, talent and anyone else who dared piss him off. His rants often ended with "I should kill you" or "you'll never work in this fucking town again." To be fair, his fury directed at various persons never lasted for very long, and after five minutes passed, he could be very nice to the same person he just condemned to the unemployment line. Many in the music business and in the media had a special true love-hate relationship with him that lasted for years.

Midway through the talk, student coordinator, Audrey Stein asked Bill to account for his stated lack of interest in helping new or unknown groups. Graham again gave the "draw" formula and further stated that no one had ever come up with a good solution on how to deal with that. He pointed out that for several years he had an audition night weekly at the Fillmore-West. Some times he would see a good band and help them in some way. Most of the bands that played the audition night did not make it beyond that initial audition. I knew personally about his audition nights at the Fillmore as two bands I managed had played there.

Bill Graham appears at Opportunity High 1973. Photo by John Klein

He concluded his two-hour talk with a long story about Santana and the Rolling Stones. The kids were riveted by Graham's every word. We all thanked him for giving the talk, and he left in an apparent good mood. I felt that Joe had something up his sleeve about this visit from "Mr. Music Business."

I knew Bill Graham from before as Gold had played several gigs for him at both Fillmore-West and at Winterland. At the last gig he called Dennis, my co-manager, and me into his office and said, "Look, I really like the band but you have to get an album going and it has to get steady air play. I am booking third bill bands now that are on the Billboard top 25 list. I really can't book Gold anymore till you get that album out." As it turned out Gold never did get a major record deal and they broke up in late 1973.

The next day Joe came in with the plan. We would make a written proposal to Graham suggesting that he support the students at Opportunity by assisting the class called the Music Business in Theory and Practice. The idea was to allow students to put on and run every aspect of a rock concert. The letter was mailed and we waited for a reply. Soon an invitation came to meet with Graham in his office so on April 24, 1973 a student delegation from the school made up of Claire Tomlinson, Jerry Cheney, Ed Dee and myself arrived to meet with Bill at his office on 11th Street in the South of Market area.

Ron Cabral in 1972
Photo by Rita
Cabral

Bill was sitting behind a glass partition, which had an old studio "ON THE AIR" sign nailed above it and was yelling furiously into a telephone. We nervously waited for 15 minutes while he continued to yell. Finally a stern and very business like looking secretary led us into his inner office. There were pictures of several rock stars on the wall. Graham seemed to be in a mellow mood as Ed Dee handed him our formal proposal.

He started to read the three-page proposal, which asked him to take a position on the community advisory board of Opportunity 2

High and also agree to become music and general arts consultant and or volunteer teacher to the school. The proposal went on to suggest that a new concept called "Summerland" be created.

Summerland would be like a minor league arena for up-and-coming bands not yet ready to play in the major league arenas. That students and music staff from Opportunity would operate and manage Summerland with help from Bill Graham's Presents. The proposal pointed out that students enrolled in the mini-course called The Music Business in Theory and Practice would earn high school credits in a variety of areas. Also all students working on the Summerland project would earn $1.75 per hour, which would qualify them for work experience, credits applicable towards their high school diplomas.

We proposed that Bimbo's 365 Club in North Beach be the site for Summerland and that 10 weekly, Friday and Saturday night dance concerts be presented. It was further stated that each band wanting to play at Summerland would have to be selected by a student booking committee unless recommended by Bill. Ideally, each show should contain one well-known group or artist, a local band with demonstrated draw ability and two new groups.

A partial band list of groups who could make bills for some of the first Summerland shows are as follows:

Nimbus

Clover

Copperhead

Seymour Light

Osceola

Gold

Butch Whacks and the Glass Packs

The Rowan Brothers

Norman Greenbaum

Barry Melton and the Fish

Redwing

Crossfire

Hoodoo Rhythm Devils

The East Bay Sharks

Wildwood

Malo

Bittersweet

The Sufi Choir

The Ducks

Midnight Sun

New Salvation Army Banned

Azteca

Mike Bloomfield

White Buffalo

Stone Ground

Cold Blood

At this point, Graham put the papers down and stared out the window for a long time. "Why me?" he asked.

Ed Dee stepped up, and said that Graham was by far the most qualified man in the community to sponsor such a project. After he finished, Bill looked at Ed silently staring at him for a couple of heartbeats.

He then quickly said, "look here's the deal if you could go out and get someone the caliber of Jerry Garcia, Paul Kantner, John Fogerty, or Carlos Santana I might make it happen." Bill ignored our blank stares and continued, "What if I told you I was going to headline Joe Stein at the Cow Palace next Friday night?—What would you think?"

Claire asked, "Who's Joe Stein?"

"Exactly", Bill said, "He's a nobody, and nobody would pay to come and see him—do you get what I am saying." He then said 10 concerts were too much and that four might be more realistic and that we would have to book all the shows without his help.

Jerry Garcia in 1968 on Haight Street. Photo by Steve Brown.

He ended the meeting by offering us "a lot of luck" and that he would be in touch. He had given a green light of sorts, but I don't think he really expected a bunch of high school kids to be able to pull any big names into the picture.

We went back to the school for a pow-wow. Bill would not put up any money unless we came up with a show we booked ourselves that had the kind of names that Bill was used to seeing. This all seemed like an impossible task for a high school teacher and a bunch of students. Claire Tomlinson said she would personally go after the Grateful Dead and she knew how to reach them. Others went after Jefferson Airplane and Santana. In the meantime I went over to see Mr. Bimbo about re-serving some dates for these possible shows.

Mr. Bimbo said, "I can give you a Friday night May 25th if you give me a $500.00 deposit." I asked him to hold that date and that I would let him know within two or three days—he only did this because he knew Bill Graham might be involved.

Two days later Tomlinson was jumping up and down while she told us she did not get the Grateful Dead, but got Jerry Garcia instead. Garcia agreed to do it only if he was billed as part of Old and In the Way a bluegrass group made up of himself, David Grisman, John Kahn, and Peter Rowan. Claire was on a roll she even booked the second bill group the Rowan Brothers. I booked the two new and local groups the Sufi Choir a 23-member singing and instrumental group who I had heard once before at a Dead concert at Winterland. The other group had just returned from a tour in India and was called Seymour Light, the lead guitar player once played with Osceola, a very good band that had appeared on bills with Gold in San Francisco and at the 1970 Vortex Festival in Oregon.

Tomlinson called Bill, and he said to go for it. The check was in the mail, and it was really happening.

Claire called Joe who was performing in New York City to tell him that his idea had taken hold. Immediately thirty students were signed up to be on the work crew.

A red business phone was installed in my classroom, which became the operations office for the new mini course. I asked Dave Pallavicini, an old friend I had met in elementary school, to make the Summerland poster. We wanted 1000 printed and 10,000 handbills. There was a circus-like atmosphere at the school. Most of the other teachers were very curious about all the comings and goings but didn't really understand that we were now working with Bill Graham—it was totally unbelievable and quite bizarre.

Just before Joe left for New York, we'd had an advertising meeting at the school, and he suggested that because Summerland was really out to help the new and unknown groups that the poster should have the little band on top and the headliner at the bottom. It made sense considering the idea for Summerland. I called Pallavicini and told him to make the poster accordingly; he was just starting to design it so he had no problem setting it up with Seymour Light at the top. Within a few days the posters were out on the streets and were being put up in storefronts and on telephone poles in places like the Haight, Berkeley, North Beach, and San Francisco State. An army of students passed out the handbills, which were miniature posters, to places all over town.

As the media started to pick up on Summerland good things started to happen. Many radio and TV stations put out advertising as public affairs announcements, which were free, and various newspapers wrote pieces on Summerland.

We were in the eye of the storm. The red phone rang in my classroom. Thinking it was another band trying to get on our list, I answered the phone. "Hi this is Summerland." The reply was, "What the fuck are you people thinking about, why the hell did you put Jerry Garcia at the bottom of the poster?" When I tried to explain Joe's idea, Bill's voice went up and he said next time ask for advice, "I am supposed to be on your advisory board, remember!" All I could picture was Bill behind that glass partition yelling at me on the phone.

The controversial
Summerland poster
by Dave Pallavicini

Things were heating up as opening night drew close.

Class began at 7:45 p.m. with the opening of the doors at Bimbo's. Three hundred people lined up to buy tickets, and they made their way in slowly. Students were selling tickets inside the ticket booth, others took tickets at the door, some students were security guards, some were stage crew, others equipment handlers. Joe's idea was a reality thanks to a bunch of so called "disenfranchised" kids from Opportunity.

The first band started to play. Garcia, Sam Cutler, and Owsley Stanley arrived early during the Sufi Choir set and were escorted back stage to their guestrooms by students on the stage crew.

Garcia was in an amiable mood and chatted freely with many of the student workers. I went over and shook his hand and thanked him for

146

helping with the project. I asked him if he had gone to school in San Francisco, he said, "oh, yeah I went to Denman Jr. High and then to Balboa—school for me was kind of painful and rough." It sounded like he didn't want to talk about it.

Jerry then walked over and spoke to Ramana Rappold the student who was selected to be the student emcee for Garcia. Ramana, a major Dead Head, calmly went up on stage at midnight and introduced Jerry and Old and In the Way to a crowd that had grown to more than 500. Old and In the Way played a great set, and the crowd applauded nicely. Most of the students working and on staff at Bimbo's were extremely happy to be part of something so unreal and yet so real—they had made history of a sort.

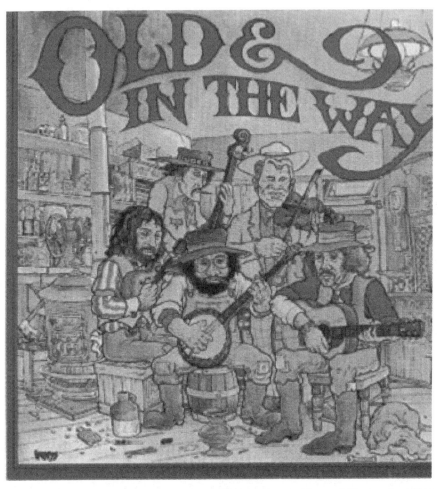

Old and In The Way. Cover Art by Greg Irons, Round Records 1974
-Courtesy of Steve Brown collection.

The next day the reality of the Music Business in Theory and Practice hit home in a big way. The red phone rang again it was Bill. He came right to the point. "Look I am losing big money on this project. You didn't do so well at the box office and you had Jerry Garcia. You will have to sell twice as many tickets at the next show or I will pull out."

I was shaken and from then on began to dread the ring of the red phone. I called a meeting of the entire Summerland staff and told them what Bill had said. I really wished Joe had been around at this time.

Claire Tomlinson really demonstrated how powerful a committed student could be when given an unlimited learning opportunity. She had already learned how to be a booking agent and had even gotten some prison gigs like San Quentin lined up for Country Joe and the All-Star band. She now was going after bigger fish.

Joe and Claire Tomlinson at Bread and Roses gig in Berkeley.
Photo Ron Cabral.

In order to try and save Summerland's future she called Joe at his hotel in New York City and explained what was going on. She then laid a heavy request on Joe. She asked him to reform Country Joe and The Fish for the second Summerland show set for June 16th. Joe thought hard about that request. He did have Barry Melton back with him at the time, and he decided to give Claire a very serious assignment over the phone. He asked her to try and pull the other Fish members together. If she could do that he would do the gig with the reformed group.

Claire tried very hard to put the Fish back together for Joe and Summerland, but the band members were all over the place and she just wasn't able to make it happen. There was also the problem that Country Joe and The Fish had so many different former members she really wasn't sure which ones to call.

So, Claire and the booking committee put together a second show quickly as Bimbo had already been paid. The next show was to headline local jazz great John Handy. Also on the bill were Butch Whacks and the Glasspacks, Norman "Spirt in the Sky" Greenbaum, and Crossfire. The show was a real variety show featuring jazz, 50's, and 70's rock with a top 40 hit artist Norman Greenbaum thrown in. I thought it would be terrific. Bill told me it seemed iffy but he let the Summerland advertising go out through his agency.

Everything seemed set, but one factor I hadn't counted on was 18-year-old naked ambition. Claire suddenly started acting like a top sergeant. She was trying to run everything by her self. She started sounding like Bill about draw, draw, and draw. I had given the students every opportunity to take this project from start to finish, but things started to get out of hand. Before anyone knew it, just days before the event, on her own, Claire had called Bill and cancelled the show.

I found out the hard way. The red phone rang. It was Bill. My palms began to sweat.

"I am gonna come over there and kill you and whoever else I need to. Number one get my fucking deposit back from Bimbo, and I'm through with

Summerland ticket

you people. No more Summerland—it's over." The intensity in his voice melted the phone in my hand. I was getting familiar with hearing an angry Bill Graham, but not like I just had. (My memory of this phone call was revived for me years later after I saw Graham in the 1991 film called *Bugsy* starring Warren Beatty and Annett Bening. In it he gives a stunning portrayal of a New York mobster - he sounded like that on the phone.) I wondered for a moment if I would ever work in this town again, although I realized he couldn't take my teaching job. Then Bill slammed the phone down in a way that made me believe that he would need a new one.

I tried to get the deposit back from Bimbo but he rightfully said no, so I took the news back to school. The staff suggested that we hold a graduation party at Bimbo's on the night of June 16th and we did just that. I was able to book Gold and Seymore Light. The only thing we thought we could do next was pass the hat at the Golden Gate Park band stand that was scheduled for that Saturday. I didn't really know if Graham ever broke kneecaps or actually killed anyone, but I didn't want to be a test case.

Bimbo's Marquee announces Opportunity High School Graduation
Party -1973. Photo by Ron Cabral

I called Joe, and he told me that he had overdosed on how weird
things had gotten with the Summerland deal and having to deal with
someone who goes off like Graham does. So it appeared to be over
with Bill making a total donation of $2,700.00. I do have to give Joe full
credit for making this whole thing with Summerland happen. It was his
idea to start with, and he just let it all happen. Joe's creation made
many kids happy, we all learned something, and it was sure fun while it
lasted. Joe left his volunteer teaching stint after Summerland, and the

school changed greatly after his departure. Joe made a difference while he was there and he touched a lot of lives.

As it turned out Graham didn't really want the money paid back, so Summerland went into rock and roll history by putting on a free concert in the park featuring Joe's friend, John Cipollina, of Quicksilver Messenger Service, with his new band Copperhead, Stoneground, and the Ducks. It was a great day in the park and Cipollina never sounded better.

John Cipollina playing with Copperhead. Photo by Lynn Baxter. From the Mike Somavilla collection

Fortunately for me, Graham got tired of trying to wring money out of a bunch of school kids, and I guess breaking my kneecaps would get him nothing. So I never heard anything else about the money or about any other dealings with Bill on this event. I never did figure out how an 18-year-old high school kid, managed to knock heads with the Czar of rock and roll and what got in to her to cancel that second gig at Bimbo's. After Summerland ended I never saw or heard from Claire again; however, I did learn later that she went on to express her talent by booking several gigs for Joe and the ALL-Star Band and other bands into prison gigs at San Quentin, Santa Rita, and Frontera Women's prison—all this prior to Bread and Roses starting up. She also was a Director for the Mill Valley Film Festival.

This did not end my contact with Bill, however, and in fact, several years after Summerland, I ran into him again in 1975. Bill appeared on a school district owned (NPR) radio station called KALW 91.7 fm on a weekly show I produced there called "The Natural High Express." Students from Opportunity and I taped music shows each week that ran on Saturday nights. I read in the paper that Bill was planning to put on a huge benefit to save sports programs in the San Francisco schools, so we invited him to come and tell us about it. I was a little worried that Bill would not accept based on our last meeting but he graciously accepted. I introduced Bill and just gave him the microphone so he could tell the audience why he was doing this. Bill explained that he had pretty much had a position to help people who wanted to raise money for something justifiable and that the money would really help a good cause.

Bill said, "Normally if those wanting a benefit could get a name artist to do a show I would help out. This time I really wanted to help the city kids and no one had to ask me. I was sick and tired of driving past ball fields and playgrounds in town and seeing no one playing on them—what the hell is going on?" At the end of the show he said something few people understood then, he said, "What if I told you I was gonna throw a party and Marlon Brando was gonna be there—would you come?" We all kind of looked at each other and shrugged our shoulders.

Last Summerland gig headlined Copperhead—It says Country Joe on the poster but he couldn't make it due to being on the road...credit Summerland Staff Art Dept.

The school district promised to pipe in the interview to as many city high schools as they could and they advertised it in the district newsletter. Bill announced on our radio show that he was going to put on a special benefit concert called **SNACK** Sunday at Kezar Stadium (the former home of the San Francisco 49ers) in Golden Gate Park - SNACK stood for San Francisco Needs Athletics, Culture and Kicks. As it turned out, 50,000 fans showed up and Bill donated $200,000 dollars to the beleaguered school sports program. At the sold out concert; Bob Dylan, The Band, Joan Baez, The Doobie Brothers, Jefferson Starship, Neil Young and Santana played one of San Francisco's greatest out-door events ever held. Also appearing at SNACK SUNDAY were several big name sports stars: Willie Mays, John Brodie and Gene Washington of the 49ers, and Track legend Jessie Owens. During a set change, one of Hollywood's greatest actors, Marlon Brando, was called out from behind the stage to make a speech to the kid's in the audience and he spoke about the American Indians being here before us and that we could learn many things from them. He then presented a check to a nervous school district official in a gray suit. Bill had a lot of friends and Marlon was one of them. Brando's appearance made the whole event totally bizarre and unbelievable to me. Well he did tell a radio audience that he was going to invite Marlon to his party.

A few weeks later one of Graham's top staff people, Zohn Artman, called me while I was in the middle of teaching a class at Opportunity to tell me that no one from the school district even bothered to thank Bill for what he had done. I told Artman I would check on that right away. I immediately called the superintendent's office and requested that they send a thank you letter to Bill and pronto. I assume they did cause I never heard anymore about it.

Maybe someone at the central office was saved from one of Bill's memorable phone calls.

10: JOE THE FAMILY MAN

Joe has had four marriages, three divorces and five kids. Joe said, "A couple of years after my Navy hitch I married Kathe Werum. We lived together briefly in Berkeley in late '65 and '66 - we broke up in'66. Kathe now lives in Maine—she still goes by the name of Kathe McDonald." I met Kathe in '65 when Joe dropped in to see me at my folk's house in Noe Valley with the stated intention that he had arrived to "break into show business."

Joe continued, "After breaking up with Kathe I married Robin Menken a few years later. We had one child, Seven Anne, who is now 35. She has been living in Los Angeles for a long time and she is a writer. I was at her birth in a hospital in San Francisco and I helped raise her. Seven is my first child and she is very special to me.

Ron Cabral

Silver and Gold

Words and music by Joe McDonald
© 1968 by Joyful Wisdom Music BMI

Dress my baby in silver and
Dress my baby in silver and
Dress my baby in silver and gold
Now, now, now, now, now.
Rubies, sapphires and diamonds
Rubies, sapphires and diamonds
Rubies, sapphires and diamonds on her hands
Now, now, now, now, now.
She don't never tell me lies
She don't go with other guys
She just wants to keep me high
Oh my baby drives me crazy.
Oh my baby drives me crazy.

Although we did have a housekeeper then I took off from the road as much as I could and acted in Robin's Improvisational-Comedy troupe in San Francisco at the Intersection Theatre. Her troupe was called the Pitschel Players and I took them with me on the road once to New York City were we played at the Bitter End.

We had a lovely home in Berkeley and we did the best we could, but things just did not work out—the divorce was costly for me and very ugly. Robin and I still talk, but we don't have much affection left for each other. I do appreciate what positive things she has done for Seven and I blame myself for much of what happened."

The cover of the Country Joe and The Fish album *Together* has a scene from the wedding and some of the guest's are on the cover. It was a very nice wedding with all the trimmings.

Joe said, "Then I married Janice Taylor and we had two kids, Devin now 25, and Tara who just turned 21. Tara just graduated from Mills College - she is a reporter for a newspaper in the Sacramento area. Devin is a certi-fied massage technician who also works as a DJ at Raves around Berke-ley and San Francisco. Devin lives on and off with his mother in

Joe & Robin Wedding Photo
Courtesy of Joe McDonald

Richmond, but most recently shared an apartment with three women in Berkeley.

When Tara was attending Mills she got some scholarship help from her mother Janice who was a Mills alumna. We lived in a very large house in the Berkeley foothills that had a beautiful view of the entire Bay Area. This marriage also ended in divorce and it was hard on all of us. I learned from this divorce to mind my own business up to a point."

"Now I have been married to Kathy Wright for 19 years and we have two kids. Emily 15 is in high school, and Ryan 12, is in middle school. Kathy is a registered nurse (RN) Labor and Delivery nurse, in a big East Bay hospital, and we are very happily married. My wife now works the most hours and I am like a housewife—I do not like the term househusband. I have been wiping asses and feeding kids for a long time, but never really understood the connection between ovulation and child support until I married a mid-wife. I am a very slow learner."

When Seven was about three or four and my daughter Denise was about the same age, Joe and I would get the kids together at birthday parties. Once we went over to Joe and Robin's house on Alcatraz Ave in Berkeley for Seven's birthday. Jane Fonda's baby was there and lot's of other kids. Everyone wore party hats and when it started to rain Joe got all the kids inside to watch a Laurel and Hardy movie.

Seven McDonald and Denise Cabral at a birthday party in 1969.
Photo by Ron Cabral.

Kathy, Joe, Ryan at 6 and Emily at 9. From McDonald family archives.

We were living in Daly City then and when we had kid's parties Joe would bring Seven over for those celebrations. Denise and Seven got a chance to get acquainted for a little while.

A few years later our son Christopher came along. I brought him over to Joe's when he was just learning how to crawl and he just took off all over the house real fast. On a particular visit Joe played some tunes for us from his *Tonight I'm Singing Just for You* album, which is pure country western—the back up band was made up of all Nashville studio musicians. I really loved that album and thought it was a shame it never got enough exposure or acceptance from the country western radio stations. Joe is a natural country singer and his name is Country. When Joe performs Woody Guthrie music he is moving towards that country direction more and more.

Years later when Cabral Christopher. was about 11, I took him to a New Year's Eve party at Joe's and we had a long talk with Barry Melton. Barry was telling us that he was studying to become a lawyer. Everyone was surprised that Barry was doing that. Chris asked me how could a famous psychedelic guitar player like Barry become a lawyer like Perry Mason. I didn't know how to answer that but Barry went on to become a lawyer just like he said he would and he became a big lawyer in Yolo County near Sacramento.

Joe and his son Ryan in 2002 at The Summer of Love anniversary gig
in San Francisco.
Photo by Ron Cabral.

Another time we all went to Joe and Janice's house in the Berkeley foothills. We had some tea, cookies and brownies there and on the way home my wife Rita started to feel a sort of far away feeling—it took her a while to come down off those special brownies. Joe maintained he didn't know what was in those brownies.

I first met Kathy McDonald at a traveling Vietnam War wall exhibit (a smaller replica of the one in Washington D.C.) in the park across from city hall in Berkeley in 1997. I was one of many readers of the names of the fallen listed on the wall. The plan was to have all 58,000 names read aloud over a 4-day period around the clock till all the names were read. Each reader read about 500 names for 30 minutes, and then was relieved by another reader. Joe was responsible for bringing the exhibit to Berkeley and he had just piloted an effort to get the

City of Berkeley to put up a plaque to those from Berkeley killed in Vietnam placed at the Veteran's Building. He also led the charge on getting the City to establish an inter-active web site about the Berkeley War dead established. I saw Joe in the park after I read the names and he told me that he was trying to get Willie Brown the Mayor of San Francisco to endorse a similar plaque for those native San Franciscan's who died in the Vietnam War put up in Justin Herman Plaza in the City. This finally occurred on Memorial Day 2001 and Joe and his friend M.L. Liebler performed at the dedication.

In 2000, I finally met Devin at the Ashkenaz club in Berkeley, at a benefit Joe was doing for medical marijuana. We had a chance to rap a bit back stage—it was a hectic scene as Wavy Gravy, Harvey Mandel and members of a band called the Cannabis Healers (Barney Doyle from the Mickey Hart Band and Terry Haggerty from Sons of Champlin) were in the room tuning up. Devin was there with his three female roommates. He is the spitting image of a young Joe—uncanny resemblance indeed.

I also met Tara a few months later at the Noe Valley Ministry in San Francisco. Tara often helps Joe sell memorabilia at gigs—CD's, t-shirts, mugs, posters and other Country Joe items. She was telling me that she was getting into public relations work and writing articles and advertising for Joe. I had a chance to speak with her a little as we were loading Joe's car after the gig—the Honda with the GIMEANF license plate on it.

Through it all Joe has always been a family oriented man as much as he could possibly be and he helped raise all 5 kids. He realized once a long time ago when he took baby Seven Anne to the hospital for some urgent medical tests that he had very strong paternal instincts, and that he felt all the same feelings any caring father would about his child. He was at the birth of all 5 young McDonald's including Ryan who was born at home. He has become like a Bing Crosby figure with adult children and some very young one's still at home. Joe has always been very attentive to all his brood and has given them as much love and care as a father can. Joe has purposely cut down on his long road trips so he can spend more time at home with the youngsters Ryan and Emily. He also stays in close contact with all the other older kids as much as possible. Often all the kids' show up at Joe's Bay Area gigs along with Kathy—it's like a real family thing. Since Kathy is a full time Nurse, Joe has taken up a domestic role. Joe says it's like being a housewife—taking care of the kids, cooking, cleaning, shopping and this goes on all the time. This is nothing new as Joe has been doing all this for along time now.

My wife Rita Cabral and our three kids...L to R: Christopher, Denise,
Rebecca and Rita - 1978.
Photo by Ron Cabral.

11: JOE AND THE VIETNAM VETS

Both Joe and I are Vietnam era veterans by virtue of our Navy service in Japan in 1960/61. I became aware of this in 1968 when I started receiving the Vietnam Era GI Bill for attending post-graduate classes at San Francisco State College. It took Joe a while longer to figure out he was actually a Vietnam era veteran. It took till 1980 for Joe to accept his status. Joe had his realization after a vet activist named Jack McCloskey told him he was a vet. Joe was torn for years between being an era veteran and being known as the author of the "Fixin'-To-Die Rag" and a leader in the anti-war movement.

Back in September 1967 I was asked to assist a vets and anti-war group in San Francisco to put on a benefit concert for Vietnam Summer an organization that wanted to draw peoples attention on the war. I had just completed a little training in organizing a show for Albatross Productions so I agreed. Thinking I knew something about booking groups I proceeded to book The New Salvation Army Banned, Darby Slick's group called Hair, Indian Head Band and Grandmother Picket's Surprise. California Hall was rented and the show was on. The only problem was that during the show Grandmother Picket's Surprise was introduced as the next band. They were not a band at all it turned out, but a troupe of naked dancers who painted their bodies with psychedelic paint. They came out dancing. Well the management called the cops who showed up in a paddy wagon. They started running around looking for them to arrest. They escaped out the back. I remember telling the officer, "We didn't know they were not a band—sorry about that." Pallavicini made the Vietnam Summer Poster thinking Grandmother Picket was a band. I found myself in several anti-war rallies over the next few years including the huge moratorium rallies held inside Golden Gate Park with my band Gold. Joe was appearing at war protest rallies all over the place with Country Joe and The Fish during those years. By 1969 Woodstock became the largest anti-war venue in the land. This was the time when we were bombarded with body counts daily on the evening news, which we watched during dinner. The Vietnam War was all around us and it lasted for years. As a Navy vet myself I was torn between being a vet and participating in anti-war events. I always felt I was doing the right thing as the war made little sense to anyone. Then my old friend Mike Riordan got killed in Nam while serving in the Merchant Marine.

Vietnam Summer poster by **Dave Pallavicini**

It was now 1980 and a blazing hot 100 degree summer day in Concord when Joe called to tell me he was coming to town to play a veterans gig. He asked if I wanted to go with him. My first thought was that it was going to be at the Concord Pavilion a new venue then that put on big shows. Joe stopped me in my tracks when he said it was going to be at a local motel near the freeway. Well I immediately said I would love to go.

About an hour later he came by the house and we drove over to a motel near the freeway. We checked in at the office and Joe asked for the room number of his contact Birch Ramsey. When we got to the room I was surprised to see about 50 vets and their wives or girlfriends. There was a big map of Vietnam over the bed and we were given a very warm welcome. Over on the nightstand was a large cake with a red and black unit flag with a skull and cross bones on it - the insignia of Ramsey's Tank Corps Unit.

Joe holds up Insignia after Motel room performance for Vets in Concord 1981. Photo by Ron Cabral.

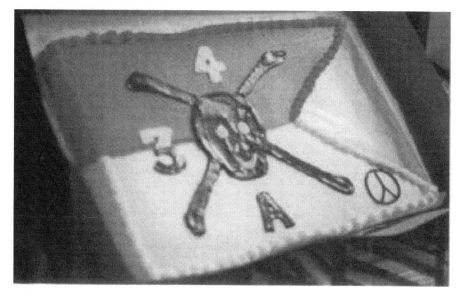

Cake at Concord Motel room - Tank Corps Unit Insignia. Photo by Ron Cabral.

Joe went to work right away taking out his guitar quickly. He then sat on the bed and started playing basically the same set he would play in a nightclub or at a concert. Joe really got their attention when he did the "Fish Cheer" and then broke into the "Fixin'-To-Die-Rag." Some of the vets couldn't believe that Joe actually came to play for them at the motel. At the conclusion of the set they really sounded off with a great round of applause. Then Joe took out some audiocassette tapes he had of the same music he just played and told them he would offer them for $5 each. Many of the vets lined up by the bed and dropped $5 into the guitar case as Joe handed them a cassette. We all had some cake and soon left the motel and headed back to my house. Joe told me that day some things about the problems many of the vets encountered when they returned home from the war. He said he realized that he had started to take up the causes of the vets and was starting to play benefits for them around the country.

For the next 23 years Joe has been consistent in his support of Vietnam vets and their causes. He has appeared at memorials, benefits, symposiums, and conventions like Veterans for Peace and Viet Nam Veterans Against the War Reunions. Joe has become knowledgeable on such issues as PTSD and Agent Orange. He started campaigns in the cities of Berkeley and San Francisco to get city officials to put up monuments to those killed in Vietnam from those cities. He has been instrumental in bringing the traveling Vietnam Wall to both Berkeley and San Francisco, in both cases the names of the over 58,000 killed were read out loud. At the dedication of the San Francisco Memorial plaque Joe sang "Mourning Blues," "Remembrance" and "Carry On."

Joe sings at San Francisco Vietnam Memorial unveiling 2001. Photo by Ron Cabral

I ran into Gerald Nicosia, a distinguished writer, at a reading he was giving at Cody's Books in Berkeley. He told me that Joe had done a benefit several years ago with poet Maxine Hong Kingston at the house of activist Jeff Mackler, in Oakland, to help him raise money to transcribe hundreds of tapes for his tome *Home to War*. His book deals with conditions the vets faced when they returned home from the war and it wasn't pretty. Nicosia said, "Joe is totally accepted and loved by all the vets I know. He is always there to do a memorial or benefit concert or just entertain at veterans' events. He is one of the guys and is never a "celebrity" amongst them. Like all the vets I know you don't try and lay any hype down on Joe, and he plays it straight with you. Like other vets I know, Joe also suggests a lot of anger just below the surface, and weariness at the injustice that goes on and nothing you can do to make a long-term difference. Vets spend a lot of time raising their kids, keeping up friendships and keeping the community together. I think when Jack McClosky told Joe that he was a vet too, he gave him a key to the identity he'd always been searching for, and maybe not too successfully in the Sixties psychedelic rock world."

Vet-activist Phil Reser who has known Joe for 25 years told me about Joe and his role with the vets. In 1990 Reser was a Board member of Swords Into Plowshares - A San Francisco Veterans Advocacy Group. I asked him what he thought when he first heard Joe's song "Fixin' to-Die- Rag" while he was serving in Viet Nam. He said, "Almost everyone in Nam knew and had heard Joe's Rag and Fish cheer. Of course it was not played on the Armed Forces radio network. When I was a grunt in 1969, all of my friends and I knew the United States was involved in one of the most controversial wars in its existence. The Vietnam War represented the first American conflict that significantly lacked support from everyone at home. This was the thing about the "Fixin'-to-Die Rag", it represented all those deeply almost unconscious thoughts and feelings about the lack of consensus regarding the U.S. involvement, and how we kids just out of high school had little hope that we might come back home alive or at least in one piece. Some of us believed that the War was necessary in protecting democracy and protecting freedoms across the world. Others believed that the U.S. had no right involving themselves in a civil war and to send our young Americans to a war whose purpose was so unclear. I heard the "Fixin'-to-Die Rag" over there and also listened to the psychedelic rock and blues like Iron Butterfly, Blind Faith, Canned Heat, The Animals - "We Gotta Get Out of This Place" was a big favorite."

I received a letter from another friend of Joe's, Vietnam veteran-activist Gordon Smith of Monterey. He told me about his Rio Americano (Sacramento) High School pal Rocky Cole who was drafted and served in the U.S. Army as a member of the 11th Light Infantry Brigade at Duc Pho. Smith said, "At a time when Joe's "Fixin' To Die Rag" played the airwaves of the world, Rocky's letters I received from Vietnam simultaneously revealed the horrible combat patrols he went on against the North Vietnamese Army and the Viet Cong. After two months into his tour Rocky wrote:

Nov 9, Gordon,...I'm looking at what I step on. About a month ago 22 of us went out. We hit a (booby trapped) 155mm artillery round, only 8 came back, the rest of the guys (medivacked out) were really torn up bad, nobody was killed but most will never walk again. I don't see any reason for it either. I've seen so many guys killed and wounded and for no good reasons. Maybe the government will realize this soon;

I've been lucky so far. I hope my luck holds out for 10 more months. Well that's all I have to tell you now.—Rock

Smith went on, "Ironically, Rocky wore beads on combat patrols which represented his free spirit like the hip San Francisco scene, as Joe wore Army fatigues in concerts while singing the grunts anthem: "Fixin'-To-Die Rag."—they were of the same brotherhood." Smith said further, "Joe's lyrics in the Rag at one point sardonically say: "Be the first one on your block to have your boy come home in a box." This lyric was nothing but a direct wake-up call to America and for those of us whom had loved ones in combat; it was a lyric that prepared us for the worse. We always cranked the volume up when it came on. We hated the message, but we respected the messenger that had the balls to sing the before unspeakable truth: Uncle Sam was killing thousands of American teen-aged boys for no logical reason. My good friend Robert Owen "Rocky" Cole, a fifth generation San Franciscan, surfer, hip cat, shirt-off-his-back friend, was stolen from his friends and family at the age of nineteen and ultimately killed by dishonest U.S. advisors, misguided U.S. policy, and Wall Street profiteering. In the depths of despair, Rocky had hoped our government would realize the senseless carnage and end the war while he was there, or that his luck would hold out for his 12-month tour. Instead he was killed in his sixth month of murderous combat at the age of twenty - too young to legally vote or even buy a beer. The family, his girlfriend, and I met his body at the Sacramento train station were he arrived in a shinny government issued aluminum box - just as Joe sang about." Rocky was killed in a NVA ambush while crawling to the aid of his wounded platoon sergeant (for which he was posthumously awarded the Silver Star for heroism). Smith was instrumental in having a memorial plaque placed at the Rio Americano High School campus in the memory of Rocky and two other of his classmates Daniel Twitty, and Terry Joslin who also died in Vietnam. At the bottom of the plaque honoring Cole, Twitty, and Joslin it is inscribed: "We graduated into the 'Summer of Love' but the winter of war soon swooped down and took you from us. One by One you left - never to come home to the places where you grew up - never to kiss your mothers and sweethearts again. You are left in our minds forever youthful, frozen in time in the tropics of the Far East and we are left with only our broken hearts and fond memories of you."

Left, Rocky Cole with beads—permission by Christine Miller-Allen; right, plaque photo by Gordon Smith

Why did Joe focus his attention on the issues of the vets in the 80s? I asked that question to Reser who said, "I think Joe was pretty much a regular Joe and understood what being an enlisted guy was like. He knew like so many of us, that there was some real bad stuff going on in this country and things needed to change. Of course Joe still gets lumped together with some 60s radicals like Jane Fonda in the minds of some vets. It helps them explain why we lost the war in Vietnam. It was the protest movement. Of course, these anti-war folks, Joe included, demoralized the troops and said bad things and smoked pot and it's all their fault and they had long hair and made free love and they had weird music and they were all commies. They made them so mad they even are today. These vets continue to stamp their feet and cry traitors. That's the right wing attitude but if you look at the history, you would know that Joe and all the other American citizens including a fair number of Vietnam veterans were just exercising their right under the Constitution, of redress and grievance, at something they felt was seriously wrong. Americans both civilian and vets don't want to admit that they were part of the process. That they elected, backed, paid for and followed the orchestrators of this disaster as it spiraled into hell. I was part of all this and have to accept my role as such."

There has been a painful emotional rift between many of the WWII vets and the Vietnam vets since the mid-70s. Even Pete Seeger and Woody Guthrie enlisted during WWII in what was seen as a righteous war and a total victory was viewed as necessary to save the world from serious evil doers. WWII was different from Korea and Vietnam because they were really considered just police actions that did not have the country behind them. Of course many WWII vets for the most part have felt a certain disdain towards the Vietnam vets, as they perceive them as losers unlike the winners they view themselves as. Korea ended in a tie and American troops have been there ever since protecting the piece of Korea that did not fall to the communists. While in Vietnam we pulled out leaving the communists to overrun the south unifying the nation under the communist regime of North Vietnam. When Joe was going around to established veterans organizations to try and organize support for Vietnam memorials in Berkeley and San Francisco he was rudely treated by some of the WWII vets he encountered. They just didn't want to deal with anything to do with the Vietnam War...

On Memorial Day of 1990 Swords to Plowshares, a vets organization, held an awards dinner at the Parc 55 Hotel in San Francisco and presented Joe an Arts and Humanities Award. This was the largest fundraiser in Swords to Plowshares 15 year history. Bill Graham had agreed to make the presentation but he had not arrived yet while Reser the emcee took the stage in front of 300 people to introduce Joe. During Reser's comments Graham arrived having raced there straight from the airport. Phil then had the honor of introducing Graham

Bill Graham, Joe, Wavy Gravy, Phil Reser above; Graham presents award to Joe—photos by Lance Woodruff

the Rock Czar who was also a highly decorated Korean War Vet. It was shocking to see both Bill and Joe wearing suits. Bill placed the award into Joe's hands and both received a standing ovation from the audience. It was a very high moment for Joe...

♦

Footnote: In August 2004 the Oakland Museum will open an exhibit on the Vietnam War. The exhibit will examine the huge impact the War had on the History of California. Joe, David Harris, Barry Romo, Ron Blitzer, Jerry Nicosia and General Wastemorland (not Westmorland) and members of the Vietnamese community were part of the original workshops for the planning of the exhibit held in 2001.

AN AFTERWORD

By Joe McDonald

The day that George Bush Sr. unleashed America's military might upon the Iraqi military in 1991; I was in San Diego at an anti-war rally attended by thousands of people. We read the names of all those killed in the Viet Nam War and I led them in the singing of the "Star Spangled Banner." I also did the "Gimme an F Cheer", and sang the "I-Feel- Like- I'm- Fixing to-Die Rag." Across the street was a man holding a sign that read, "Give War a Chance."

We then began to march, and after several blocks the ranks became disorganized. I started monitoring when some young kids, looking like punks or anarchists, set fire to an American flag. I quickly took it out of their hands and put it out. They wanted me to give it back to them. I told them I was keeping it, as it was not for burning. I ended up taking the flag home to Berkeley and kept in the basement. When I was in boot camp with the Navy I was never taught how to properly dispose of a flag.

A few years ago, I did a rally for those who fought in or protested the Vietnam War in Berkeley. A young man, about 20, was wearing his fathers Army jacket. He was given an American flag to hold during the ceremony and he kept dragging it on the ground. I walked over to him and told him it was not right to do that. He said, "This is just a piece of cloth to me." I stared at him and told him to hold it up, which he did.

That day we also flew the South Vietnamese flag for the first time at Sproul Plaza on the UC Berkeley campus.

On Veterans Day in 1995, the City of Berkeley Veterans Memorial Building was filled to overflowing. The crowd had come to witness the unveiling of the Berkeley Vietnam Veterans Memorial. The memorial consisted of a plaque listing the names of the twenty-two citizens who died in Vietnam. Another component of the memorial was the first interactive on-line Vietnam memorial, where anyone around the world could see photographs and other graphics connected with the lives of those claimed in that war. Visitors to the web site could also leave their own sentiments for all to share.

The Berkeley History Museum, housed inside the Veterans Building, had hundreds of artifacts from the war on display. A large red, white and blue bunting draped the building itself.

Among those gathered for the dedication were those who fought in Vietnam, and those who opposed the war. A Vietnam Veterans of America Color Guard, with honorary members of the South Vietnamese military, presented not only the American flag, but also the South Vietnamese flag. A Buddhist priest, so often the symbol of anti-war sentiment in both countries offered a meditation. Berkeley Mayor, Shirley Dean, wept openly as she read her speech apologizing to the families and friends present for the long delay in honoring these Berkeley citizens who died for their country.

There was a magical quality to the day. There was no anger or hostility, just complete agreement that blaming soldiers for war is like trying to blame fire fighters for fires. There was the sound of weeping as the crowd remembered and honored the lives lost in a cause most Americans, including the chief architect of the war, Secretary of State Robert McNamara, still does not claim to fully understand.

An obviously distraught woman struggled to bring her self to enter the memorial building to look at the artifacts. She was once a member of the Berkeley Vietnam era Draft Board and she was attempting to summon the courage to look upon the photographs and medals of the men she sent into battle, never to return.

How could an event like this take place in the city known to the world as The Peoples Republic of Berkeley, a place famous for the Vietnam War protests of the 60's and 70's. How could this dedication take place across the street from the same City Park known back then as Ho Chi Minh Park?

I was the person responsible for suggesting that the Berkeley memorial be built. It was as Country Joe that I earned world fame during the Vietnam era for writing and singing a song whose chorus is: "and it is 1,2,3 what are we fighting for? Don't ask me I don't give a damn. Next stop is Viet Nam - and its 5,6,7 open up the pearly gates. There ain't no time to wonder why—Whoopee - we're all gonna die." This was the same song I sang on the stage at Woodstock in 1969, in front of 400, 000 people, and for audiences all over the world ever since. I am an honorably discharged Vietnam era Veteran having served 3 years in the Regular Navy. I also grew up in Southern California with American Communist party members as parents. I had an early realization that not all Americans agree on things. Having had both these experiences in my background left me feeling victimized. I had no love for the leaders of the American military or the American left—I was not enamored or mystified by either entity. A life mission did emerge from these experiences that I was never to abandon—1.Dedication to the cause of justice. 2. A dream of peace. 3. To try and help those who cannot defend themselves.

By the time Saigon fell to the North Vietnamese and Viet Cong forces in 1975, I along with millions of others was emotionally drained and exhausted. I wanted to forget America's longest and most controversial war and get on with my life. That plan worked well for about 6 years, until the phone started ringing with requests from Vietnam veterans for my help securing benefit programs for those with war related problems. I answered this call and began a journey that eventually led me to the dedication of the Berkeley Vietnam Veterans Memorial fourteen years later.

In 1981, I managed to forget I was a military veteran and saw myself as a rock star that helped veterans. It wasn't until the late, veteran activist; Jack McCloskey reminded me that I was also a vet that I began to look at myself in a new way. I had the realization that I was just as guilty of helping conduct the war, as I was of trying to stop the war - and I found this to be a terrible blow to my ego. After this I began to talk almost exclusively of my military experiences and I identified with veterans and military personnel so much so that I was driving my family and friends a bit crazy.

I read everything I could on the subject of the Vietnam War. I began to get involved in many Vietnam Veterans events taking place all over the country. I came to Washington, D.C. dressed in Navy whites, to stand alongside members of Vietnam Veterans Against the War (VVAW). This was to protest action against the Veterans Administration's neglect of Agent Orange victims, Post Traumatic Stress Disorder, and other war related problems among Veterans and their families.

During our protest march in D.C., we paused for a moment at the then construction site of the black marble Vietnam Veterans Memorial, the product of Vietnam veteran Jan Scruggs and architect Maya Lin. Prior to this moment I had never thought about a War Memorial. But this experience got me thinking—it was perhaps my first post-war thought about the problem of healing from the War.

Soon after the visit to Washington, I was back home in Berkeley working in my garden. My neighbor was also working in his garden so we struck up a conversation, and of course, I went on and on about the Vietnam War. He then quietly told me that his son was killed in the war. I was totally stunned. I was not aware that I had ever even met someone who lost a son in that war. Now I had. It struck me that I also had a son, and that fact magnified my sense of compassion. Not long after this chance encounter with my neighbor, I was in Washington, D.C. again and went to the then finished Vietnam Veterans Memorial. I took a photograph of my neighbor's son's name and made a rubbing of the name. I brought the photo and rubbing back to my neighbor and his wife. It was a sad and loving experience talking to them about the death of their son. I discovered that a mistake had been made identifying him as a resident of New York (he had graduated from West Point, his last address prior to his death) and as such was going to be left off the California State Vietnam War Memorial in Sacramento. I was able to facilitate his name going on the California memorial. I noticed that we immediately all felt some closure and healing.

I soon found out that there were many debates in the veteran's community about the spending of great amounts of money on Monuments as opposed to the spending of money on veteran's services. I started thinking about that and many other related issues. I found that I did not feel guilty about my military service and at the same time felt no remorse over my protesting the war: I felt I had the right as a military veteran and a citizen to express my self under the first amendment.

I realized that my generation has not been allowed to grow up together and felt bad that some of my peers had never had the experience of going to rock dances and love ins in the 60s. Since I was a vet, a hippie and a known anti-war protester - who never lacked respect for the GI's - I had entrée into both worlds. I began to see the biggest difference was between the individuals who did nothing during the war and those who did do something. Those motivated to serve joined the military or the anti-war movement. Others joined the Red Cross or some other public service. Those motivated to make a moral stand sometimes left the country at great sacrifice and government intimidation, some became conscientious objectors or did hard jail time for refusing the draft. Others just dropped out and became hippies to be disowned by their parents.

The vast majority of the 50 million people making up the Vietnam generation did nothing but wait the War out. Ten million people, nine million men and one million women, served in the Vietnam era military and several million were in the peace movement or the counterculture, as it is sometimes called. Many of the people who did nothing were able to move up the social economic ladder into positions of power and leadership, leaving those who experienced the trauma of the era on the outside looking in.

In 1997, Jan Scruggs from the Washington, D.C. memorial association, offered to bring a new one-half scale replica of the D.C. Vietnam Veterans Memorial, called "The Wall That Heals" to Berkeley. The wall was to be displayed in the very park once called Ho Chi Minh Park, during protests held there during the war. The wall was to be available 24 hours a day. I arranged a program to have all 58,000 names on it read around the clock. At one point I thought that this would be impossible to accomplish given the resources and overwhelming logistics—I thought about aborting the idea, then several large donations came in and the Mayor's right hand woman Tamlyn Bright took over. Bright had a Vietnam War death in her own family. She answered every phone call and assigned every volunteer reader a time period of 30 minutes to read the names. Hundreds of people from Berkeley and all over the Bay Area volunteered to read, and Bright's answering machine was so full she could not even call them back. One group that really helped a great deal was the UC Berkeley ROTC unit. They came out in uniform and were there day and night the entire time. The program ended with a bagpiper playing "Amazing Grace" as the names of Merchant Mariners who died in the war were read. No one who attended was the same when they left. I could not help but think that had Richard Nixon and Robert McNamara been able to envision such a ceremony 30 years ago, their policies would have been much different. Happily the success of this traveling wall went on to appear in many other cities around the country.

At times I have resisted my connection to the Vietnam War. It has been consistently bad for business and I have been warned and cautioned by many of my peers for constantly bringing up the issues of the Vietnam War in my songs and in my talking to my audiences. Over the years I have accepted this as my fate. Since the time I sang "I-Feel-Like-I'm-Fixin'-to-Die Rag" at Woodstock I cannot escape a connection with the Vietnam War. Whether or not I chose to make Vietnam a focus of my life, it seems to have chosen me. My efforts to help veterans and the country heal from the war have been both reviled and honored, just like the war itself. There were times when I thought I would lose my mind. The worst of times came for me during the wars in El Salvador and Nicaragua. Extremists on the Nation's political left and right wings squandered huge resources while Vietnam Vets suffered in VA hospitals, on the streets, or in their homes with families sharing their burdens with little outside help or support.

To America's credit we finally seem, at the turn of the Century, to finally be healing and accepting the fact the Vietnam War, as McNamara now suggests, was a horrible mistake. It was certainly not the fault of those who fought the war or those who resisted it.

Joe and Pete Seeger discuss "Fixin to Die Rag" in Berkeley 1972.
Photo by Ron Cabral

Joe in 1998. Photo by Tom Weller

COMPLETE DISCOGRAPHY AND MOVIE CREDITS

With Blair Hardman

PVT Pressing "The Goodbye Blues" 1964

Xmas Present "The Goodbye Blues" 1969

PIC 3009 "The Early Years" 1980

With Country Joe and The Fish

EP's

Rag Baby RAG 1001 Talking Issue #1 (Peter Krug B Side) October 1965

Rag Baby RAG 1002 Country Joe and The Fish (3 Songs) June 1966

Rag Baby RAG 1003 Resist! (3 Songs for the FTA Show) Jane Fonda Cover May 1971 Rag Baby RAG 1008 Collector's Items: The first 3 EP's July 1981

Vanguard VSD 79244 Electric Music for the Mind and Body April 1967

Vanguard VSD 79266 I Feel Like I'm Fixin' to Die November 1967

Vanguard VSD 79277 Together August 1968

Vanguard VSD 79299 Here We Are Again July 1969

Vanguard VSD 6545 Greatest Hits December 1969

Vanguard VSD 6555 C. J. Fish May 1970

Vanguard SD 27/26 Life and Times of Country Joe and The Fish November 1971

Fantasy FAN 9530 Reunion June 1977

Vanguard VCD 111/12 Collected Country Joe and The Fish 1988

Vanguard VCD 139/40-2 Live! Fillmore West 1966 May 1996

45's

Vanguard VRS 35052 Not-So-Sweet Martha/Masked Marauder 1967

Vanguard VRS 35059 Janis/Janis (instrumental) 1967

Vanguard VRS 35061 Who Am I/Thursday 1967

Vanguard VRS 35068 Rock and Roll Music Parts 1 and 2 1968

Vanguard VRS 35090 Here I Go Again/Baby, You're Driving Me Crazy 1969

Vanguard VRS 35112 I Feel Like I'm Fixin' to Die Rag/Maria 1970

Rag Baby RAG 102 Peace on Earth/Santa Claus Rag 1983

Other Albums

Cotillion SD 3-500 Woodstock July 1970

ABC ABCS 0C19 Zachariah (Soundtrack) November 1972

MCA 262 011006 More American Graffiti 1979

Vanguard VSD 17/18 Greatest Folk Singers November 1984

Atlantic 2-82618 Best of Woodstock 1994

As Country Joe McDonald

LP's

Vanguard VSD 6544 Thinking of Woody Guthrie December 1969

Vanguard VSD 6557 Tonight I'm Singing Just for You March 1970

Vanguard VSD 79314 Hold On It's Coming April 1971

Vanguard VSD 79315 War, War, War October 1971

Vanguard VSD 79316 Incredible Live! February 1972

Vanguard VSD 79328 Paris Sessions September 1973

Vanguard VSD 79348 Country Joe December 1974

Vanguard VSD 85/86 Essential Country Joe 1975

Fantasy FAN 9495 Paradise With an Ocean View October 1975

Fantasy FAN 9511 Love is a Fire August 1976

Fantasy FAN 9525 Goodbye Blues April 1977

Fantasy FAN 9544 Rock and Roll Music from the Planet Earth 02/78

Fantasy FAN 9586 Leisure Suite December 1979

Rag Baby RAG 2001 Into the Fray 1981

Rag Baby RAG 1012 On My Own September 1981

Animus 1017/F-1 Animal Tracks August 1983

Rag Baby RAG 1018 Childs Play 1983

Rag Baby RAG 1019 Peace on Earth 1984

Rag Baby RAG 1024/25 Vietnam Experience October 1986

Fantasy FCD 7709 Classics 1989

Vanguard VCD 119/20 The Best of Country Joe McDonald 1990

Rag Baby/Ryko RAG 1028 Superstitious Blues 1991

Rag Baby/Shannachie RAG 1029 Carry On March 1995

Rag Baby/Big Beat RAG 1030 Something Borrowed, Something New May 1998

Woronzow/Rag Baby WOO 33 Eat Flowers and Kiss Babies (with The Bevis Frond) June 1999

Rag Baby RAG 1032 WWW.COUNTRYJOE.COM October 2000

Hance JCT 762001 I Feel Like I'm Fixin' to Sing Some Songs...October 2000

Akarma (Italy) 4 CD boxed set collector's edition A REFLECTION ON CHANGING TIMES—Tonight I'm Singing Just For You - Hold On It's Coming—War War War—Paris Sessions...October 2001

Arkama (Italy) THE RAG BABY EP's—collector's vinyl edition box set...November 2001

Rag Baby 1034 Crossing Borders—The Poetry of M.L. Liebler and the Music of Country Joe McDonald...2002

45's

Vanguard VRS 35150 Hang On/Hand of Man (from VSD 6555) 1973

Vanguard VRS 35161 Fantasy/I Seen a Rocket 1973

Vanguard VRS 35181 Doctor Hip/Satisfactory 1974

Vanguard VRS 35184 Chile/Jesse James 1975

Fantasy FAN 758 Breakfast for Two/Lost My Connection January 1976

Fantasy FAN 765 Save the Whales! /Oh, Jamaica April 1976

Fantasy FAN 780 Love is a Fire/I Need You 1976

Fantasy FAN 814 Coyote/Southern Cross March 1978

Fantasy FAN 822 Bring Back the Sixties, Man/Sunshine 1976

Fantasy FAN 876 Private Parts/Take Time Out 1980

Rag Baby 01 Voyage of the Good Ship Undersize (1_) 1983

Other LP's

Cotillion SO 3-500 Woodstock July 1970

Vanguard VSD 79304 Quiet Days in Clichy (Soundtrack) October 1970

AIR A-1038 Gas-s-s-s (Soundtrack) 1970

ODE 77008 Celebration at Big Sur April 1971

Vanguard VSD 35/36 Greatest Songs of Woody Guthrie 1972

Warner Bros. WB 852586 Tribute to Woody Guthrie Part 2 May 1972

Fantasy FAN 79007 Bread and Roses Festival of Acoustic Music 1980

Bootlegs

Woodstock Barry's Jam (Country Joe and The Fish)

Fillmore East Last Days/Hold On It's Coming (Country Joe)

Kralingen Festival Freedom/She's a Bird/Sweet Lorraine/For No Reason

Movies, TV, and Stage

Changeover (Stage, 1965) Written by Fred Hayden, directed by Nina Serrano. Anti-Vietnam war play performed at San Francisco State

University and UC Berkeley. Music by CJM, performed by Barry "The Fish" Melton and CJM. Score includes the song "Who Am I."

A Day in the Life of...(TV documentary, 1967) Directed by Robert Zagone. A film about Country Joe and The Fish.

How We Stopped the War (Documentary short, 1967) Directed by David Peoples. Follows Country Joe and The Fish on its way to an anti-Vietnam War rally. 29 min.

Revolution (Documentary, 1969) Directed by Jack O'Connell. Life among the hippies. Re-released in 1996, with later material added, as The Hippie Revolution. 90 min.

Monterey Pop (Documentary, 1969) Directed by D. A. Pennebaker. The film of the big rock show. 88 min.

Woodstock (Documentary, 1970) Directed by Michael Wadleigh. The film of the even bigger rock show. 184 min.

Quiet Days in Clichy (Denmark, 1970) Directed by Jens Jørgen Thorsen. Lisbet Lundquist, Elizabeth Reingaard, Wayne Rodda. Based on the book by Henry Miller. Music. 100 min.

Gas-s-s-s (1970) Directed by Roger Corman. Bud Cort, Cindy Williams, Ben Vereen, Talia Coppola (Shire). Poison gas kills everyone over 30 in one of the weirdest movies you ever saw. Edgar Allan Poe on a motorcycle! Country Joe and The Fish contribute music and appear briefly, credited as "Johnny and the Hurricanes." 79 min.

Que Hacer? (Chile, 1970) Directed by Saul Landau, Nina Serrano, and Raul Ruiz. Sandy Archer. Chronicles the atmosphere of revolution and repression on the eve of the election of Salvador Allende as president of Chile. Music directed by CJM performed by Los Jaivas, Gold and CJM who also appears in the film.

Zachariah (1971) Directed by George Englund. John Rubenstein, Pat Quinn, Don Johnson, Country Joe and The Fish, Elvin Jones, New York Rock Ensemble, The James Gang, Dick Van Patten. A surrealistic musical Western, another of the weirdest movies you ever saw. Country Joe and The Fish play the Crackers, an outlaw band. 93 min.

The Omega Man (1971) Directed by Boris Sagal. Charlton Heston, Rosalind Cash. This time germ warfare kills everyone. There's a clip from Woodstock and guess who is in it? 98 min.

Holland Pop - Country Joe solo (Bootleg, 1972) Film of the Kralingen Festival that apparently circulates underground. If anyone has more information, let us know.

Tricks (Short, 1973) Directed by Gregory Pickup. Hybiscus and the Cockettes, Allen Ginsburg. Title song "Tricks Is Made for Kids" written and performed by CJM.

Ovid's Metamorphoses (Stage, 1976?) Directed by Paul Sills. Leslie Ann Warren, Robin Menken. Performed at the Mark Tapper Forum in Los Angeles. Music written by CJM, performed by David Cohen and CJM.

More American Graffiti (1979) Directed by B.W.L. Norton. Candy Clark, Bo Hopkins, Ron Howard, Paul Le Mat, Mackenzie Phillips, Charles Martin Smith, Cindy Williams. The Grafitti gang faces the 60s. A pickup version of Country Joe and The Fish plays "Fixin' To Die" (what else?) in the "Fillmore" scenes. 111 min.

Secret Agent (Documentary about Agent Orange 1983) Directed by Jackie Ochs. Produced by Green Mountain Post Films - Music Produced and Performed by Country Joe Music.

The New Right (Documentary, 1983) Title Song by Country Joe - Performed by Country Joe Directed by Saul Landau. Music.

Vietnam Experience (Documentary, 1987) Directed by Daniel Keller and Joe McDonald. A long form music video combining my war songs with Vietnam footage. 29 min.

Berkeley in the Sixties (Documentary, 1990) Directed by Mark Kitchell. Footage from How We Stopped the War, "Fixin' to Die" and "Death Sound Blues" on the soundtrack. 120 min.

Pepsi "Woodstock" commercial (1993) As himself.

Tales of the City (TV miniseries, 1993) Directed by Alistair Reid. Olympia Dukakis, Donald Moffat, Chloe Webb, Marcus D'amico. Cameo appearance as "Joaquin." 360 min.

Animaniacs (TV series, 1994) Episode 59, "Woodstock Slappy." Produced by Steven Spielberg.

For more information on Country Joe visit www.countryjoe.com

Special thanks to the following who helped in more ways than one...

Rita Cabral, Kathy McDonald, Phil Elwood, Carole Vernier, Herb Caen, John Wasserman, Bob McDonald, Dorothy Moscowitz, Dave Pallavicini, Noel Blincoe, Phil Reser, Lee Houskeeper, Mike Somavilla, Larry Parmenter, Ralph Solonitz, Gerry Nicosia, Bill Graham, Ted Samuel, Bill Belmont, Barry Melton, David Cohen, Jon Hendricks, Tom Weller, Ben Fong-Torres, ED Denson, Joan Wallace, Dennis Cabral, Ed Scott, Sebastian Nicholson, Rod Albin, Sal Delgado, Marcia Perlstein, Gordon Smith, Miguel Rodriguez, Wolfgang Reuther, Richard Hughes, Bruce Latimer, Jill Goetz, Alan Rinzler, Shelley Duncan, David Gross, Michael Simmons, Mick Skidmore, Ed Lyngar, Sam Andrew, Tom Wilkes, Tim Thomas, Steve Brown, Lynn Baxter, John Klein, John Koenig, Rob Bleetstein, Mark Weiman, Marshall Berman, Christine Miller-Allen, Leah Garchik, Sarah Crump, Tim Murphy, Shel Horowitz, Gene Anthony, Dave Diamond.

Index

Gregory, Bill, 22, 25, 37
Grisman, David, 144
Grootna, 52
Grossman, Albert, 64
Gurley, James, 64, 68
Gut, 58, 60
Guthrie, Arlo, 100
Guthrie, Woody, viii, 9, 164,
    180, 195, 197
Haggerty, Terry, 166
Hair, 169
Handy, John, 151
Harris, David, 182
Havens, Richie, 100
Hefner, Hugh, 99
Helms, Chet, 46, 48, 55, 77
Hendricks, Jon, 133, 134, 201
Hendrix, Jimi, 59, 106, 132
Hirsh, Gary "Chicken", 74, 87,
    89, 104, 105
Holly, Buddy, 8
Hooker, John Lee, 51
Hope, Bob, 18
Hot Tuna, 51, 65, 107, 116
Houskeeper, Lee, 201
Hudson, Rock, 40
Hughes, Richard, 82, 201
Indian Head Band, 169
Instant Action Jug Band, 74
Iron Butterfly, 107, 177
Jefferson Airplane, 46, 50, 54,
    77, 106, 114, 143
Jethro Tull, 99
Johnson, Don, 103, 199
Johnson, J.J., 8
Jones, Spike, 9
Joplin, Janis, 48, 51, 52, 54, 61,
    69, 99, 106, 114

Joslin, Terry, 179
Judge Crater Memorial Blues
    Band, 49
Kahn, John, 144
KALW radio, 156
Kameny, Paul, 47
Kandel, Lenore, 44
Kantner, Paul, 142
Kapner, Mark, 74, 103
Karpen, Julius, 48
Kaukonen, Jorma, 103, 107,
    108
Kay, John, 86
Kerouac, Jack, viii, 40
Keystone Korner, 53, 65
Kingston Trio, 13
Kingston, Maxine Hong, 175
KMPX, 46, 47, 59
Kozmic Blues Band, 56
KSAN, 46
Kulberg, Andy, 107
Landau, Saul, 51, 198, 200
Laspina, Phil, 127
Latimer, Bruce, 201
Leary, Timothy, 44
Led Zeppelin, 78, 114
Leese, Howard, 132
Lewis, Jerry Lee, 8
Lin, Maya, 187
Little Richard, 8, 13
Loose Gravel, 61, 64
Lyngar, Ed, 201
MacArthur, Douglas, 15
Mackler, Jeff, 175
Main Squeeze, 61
Malo, 65, 121, 141
Mandel, Harvey, 166
Marshall, Jim, 75, 98

205

Rebel, 4, 5
Redding, Otis, 59, 106
Redwing, 141
Reser, Phil, 176, 181, 201
Reuther, Wolfgang, 201
Rexroth, Kenneth, 40
Riordan, Mike, 170
Robertson, Mary, 122
Rodriguez, Miguel, 201
Rogers, Richard, 8
Rolling Stone, 113, 114, 138
Romo, Barry, 182
Rowan, Peter, 144
Rubin, Jerry, 44
Rumney, Ron, 47
Salvation Army Banned, 48,
  60, 141, 169
San Francisco Mime Troupe,
  136
Santana, Carlos, 107, 108, 121,
  142
Santana, George, 121
Saunders, Richard, 102
Schrager, Carl, 102
Scott, Ed, 65, 66, 120, 201
Seale, Bobby, 49
Seeger, Pete, 9, 180, 191
Serrano, Nina, 80, 197, 198
Seymour Light, 140, 144, 145
Shankar, Ravi, 106
Sheen, Martin, 115
Sinclair, Robin, 51, 66, 120
Sire Records, 50
Slick, Darby, 169
Slick, Grace, 107
Smith, Gordon, 177, 179, 201
SNACK Sunday, 157
Snyder, Gary, 40

Solonitz, Ralph, 201
Somavilla, Mike, 63, 155, 201
Southern Comfort, 68
Stalin, Joseph, 1, 35
Stanley, Owsley, 146
Starr, Ringo, 108
Steel, Bob, 102
Stein, Audrey, 137
Stein, Joe, 142
Steppenwolf, 86
Sterba, James, 82
Stoneground, 52, 154
Stones, 46, 114
Strachwitz, Chris, 74
Strawberry Alarm Clock, 107
Strong, Ted, 128
Sufi Choir, 141, 144, 146
Sullivan, Ed, 99, 101
Summerland, 140, 145, 146,
  149, 150, 151, 152, 153, 154,
  156, 157
Taylor, Janice, 161
Teagarden, Jack, 8
Ten Years After, 51, 115
The Albatross, 47, 48, 58, 59
The All-Star Band, 108, 135
The Animals, 177
The Band, 114, 158
The Berkeley String Quartet,
  37, 39
The Blues Project, 107
The Charlatans, 64
The Doobie Brothers, 158
The Doors, 46, 47
The Ducks, 141
The East Bay Sharks, 141
The Greek Theatre, 115
The Mills Brothers, 18

Ron "The Squid" Cabral
Started using "The Squid" as a performing name in 2003 after performing with Country Joe on a Bay Area TV show. "We were introduced as Country Joe and The Squid."
Photo By Rita Cabral

ABOUT THE AUTHOR

Ron Cabral a native of San Francisco and graduate of San Francisco State University became a teacher in 1965 and later a middle school principal with the San Francisco public schools serving for 35 years. Between the years 1967 and 1973 while teaching and starting a family he became deeply involved in the emerging music revolution-taking place in his hometown of San Francisco. He promoted concerts and managed a few rock bands some of which played at Fillmore-West and Winterland for rock czar Bill Graham. A trombone player and percussionist since his youth he had occasion to record with Gold and play briefly with Country Joe and The All-Stars.

Ron met Joe McDonald (the subject of Country Joe and Me) while serving in the U.S. Navy in 1960.

Ron is married with 3 grown children and 3 grandchildren. He lives in Concord, California. He is currently working with a German rock label called Worldinsound and is writing his second book on a his life as a career dean and principal inside the inner-city public schools from 1984 to 2001.